POST Entry Level Law Enforcement Test Battery (PELLETB) Review

Printed in the United States of America

Table of Contents

About Trivium Test Prep

Trivium Test Prep uses industry professionals with decades worth of knowledge in the fields they have mastered, proven with degrees and honors in law, medicine, business, education, military, and more to produce high-quality test prep books such as this for students.

Our study guides are specifically designed to increase ANY student's score, regardless of his or her current scoring ability. At only 25% - 35% of the page count of most study guides, you will increase your score, while significantly decreasing your study time.

How to Use this Guide

This guide is not meant to reteach you material you have already learned or waste your time on superfluous information. We hope you use this guide to focus on the key concepts you need to master for the test and develop critical test-taking skills. To support this effort, the guide provides:

- Practice questions with worked-through solutions
- Key test-taking tactics that reveal the tricks and secrets of the test
- Simulated one-on-one tutor experience
- Organized concepts with detailed explanations
- Tips, tricks, and test secrets revealed

Because we have eliminated "filler" or "fluff", you will be able to work through the guide at a significantly faster pace than other prep books. By allowing you to focus ONLY on those concepts that will increase your score, study time is more effective and you are less likely to lose focus or get mentally fatigued.

Introduction

Contrary to popular belief, working in law enforcement is not simply about chasing criminals, fast driving, and shooting. In fact, most law enforcement officers spend the majority of their days writing and talking to people. They talk to supervisors, dispatchers, lawyers and judges, the public at large, and to criminals, before, during, and even after arrest. How an officer speaks, writes, and otherwise communicates to others is a very important part of police work. Arguably, it is the most important part.

Reading also plays an important role in a law enforcement officer's duties. Officers spend a great deal of time reading reports, statutes, case law, memos and policy changes, correspondence from the district attorney's office, as well as news reports affecting the community served and policing in general. Understanding the reading materials' content is vital; it may dictate job parameters and how the work can, or cannot, be done.

Communication is essential to a law enforcement officer. Communicating correctly can be the difference of whether or not an officer succeeds in a law enforcement career.

To ensure prospective officers are more likely to succeed, the California Police Officer Standards and Training (POST) created an aptitude test for the law enforcement entry level position to measure test takers' writing and reading abilities. For nearly 40 years, the POST Entry Level Law Enforcement Test Battery (PELLETB) has been used to determine the likelihood of a test taker's success in law enforcement. Passing the PELLETB is your first step to becoming a law enforcement officer in California. It is the gateway for admittance into the basic academy, where you will learn about police procedure and the law. The PELLETB is a measure of your communication skills and does not cover police procedure; that is covered in the academy.

This study guide contains a concise but comprehensive review of all sections tested on the PELLETB examination. It also includes two practice exams comprised of 105 multiple-choice questions, plus 22 bonus questions, answers, and explanations. Inside, you will also find tips, tricks, and comprehensive explanations for each testing area, along with scenario-style questions related to law enforcement written from the perspective of an expert who is experienced in the field, rather than simply in the style of a generalized English and grammar course. Appendix A and Appendix B both contain study words related to law enforcement to improve spelling and vocabulary, and Appendix C is comprised of prefixes, suffixes, and root words.

Congratulations! You're on your way to improving your English language skills and success on the PELLETB.

Test Format and Strategies

Taking a test can be stressful. Test anxiety is often created by "not knowing"—not knowing what to expect from the testing environment, rules for taking the test, test structure, or what the test covers. Knowing what to expect can help eliminate much of that stress. The following information identifies and defines many unknowns related to the PELLETB, and provides strategies for managing multiple-choice questions.

Format

The PELLETB is a 2½ hour, 105 multiple-choice question examination. It measures reading and writing aptitude over three sections. The first section focuses on writing language ability and tests writing clarity, vocabulary, and spelling. The second section tests reading language ability through reading comprehension. The third section of the exam focuses on reasoning ability. All of the questions are multiple-choice except for the CLOZE test, which employs a fill-in-the-blank format.

Writing

The writing section of the exam is divided into three 15-question subtests as outlined below.

1. *Clarity* – Tests grammar and ability to write concisely and with clarity.

    - The questions are presented as two sentences. You will be prompted to identify and select the sentence that is most clearly and correctly written.

    - This subtest only includes the most common grammatical errors, which will be discussed later in this review.

2. *Spelling* – Tests ability to spell commonly misspelled words.

    - The questions are presented in the form of a sentence with a word missing, designated by a blank space. Keeping the sentence context in mind, you must choose the correctly spelled word option from the list of answer choices.

    - There is no specific list of words this subtest pulls from, so it is good to study as many common words related to law enforcement as possible. A list of words to study for spelling and vocabulary is included at the end of this review.

3. *Vocabulary* – Tests ability to understand words commonly used in law-enforcement-related documents and communications.

    - The questions are presented as sentences with one word underlined. You will be prompted to choose the most accurate synonym or definition, given the sentence context, from the answer choices.

    - There is no specific list of words this subtest pulls from, so it is good to study as many common words related to law enforcement as possible. A list of words to study for spelling, vocabulary, and common prefixes, suffixes, and root words is included at the end of this review.

Reading

The reading section of the exam is divided into two subtests as outlined below.

1. *Reading Comprehension* – Tests ability to read and understand what is being communicated in short- and moderate-length passages.

    - The questions are presented after the passage in the form of a "question stem" followed by several answer choices. There will likely be multiple question stems related to one passage. You will be prompted to select answer choices based on the information contained in the passage.

    - This subtest only covers common concepts. All of the information needed to answer questions is contained within the passage.

    - This subtest has 20 multiple-choice questions.

2. *CLOZE* – Tests English language proficiency in conjunction with the context of an entire passage.

    - The questions are presented as blank spaces throughout a moderate-length passage. Only the first and last sentences of the passage are complete. In between those sentences, every seventh word is removed from the passage and replaced with a set of dashed lines. Each dash represents one letter contained in the deleted word.

    - You will be prompted to determine the missing word and fill in the blanks from your own vocabulary and based on the context of the passage.

- There ***may*** be more than one correct choice to fill in a specific blank, but each word choice must be logical and fit within the context of the passage.
- All removed words can be deduced from the context. This subtest tends to be one of the more difficult sections for test takers.
- This subtest has 40 fill-in-the-blank style questions.

Reasoning

The reasoning section of the exam measures ability to relate various pieces of information. It is divided into several 16-question multiple-choice subtests including:

1. *Ordering* – Tests ability to place information in order based on the relationship between given items.
    - The question provides several pieces of information. It then prompts you to analyze the information and determine relationships in order to determine the correct answer.
2. *Grouping* – Tests ability to identify and group similar items, or separate dissimilar items, based on their relationship to one another.
    - Questions prompt you to analyze the groupings and use commonalities to establish the correct answer.
3. *Pattern Recognition* – Tests ability to identify and complete a pattern, series, or sequence.
    - Questions prompt you to analyze the information and use patterns to determine the correct answer choice.

Five Quick Tips for Tackling Multiple-choice Questions

Many people believe multiple-choice tests are easier than other test formats because the answer is provided within a group of choices. But, multiple-choice tests can be much more difficult than expected for the unprepared test taker. Multiple-choice test creators spend considerable time formulating answer choices designed to be distractions. One commonly used example is the "red herring." In the context of a multiple-choice test, a red herring is an answer choice intended to lead test takers to a false conclusion through distraction. Now, you might be wondering why testers wish to mislead you. The truth is they don't, but they do wish to test your ability to understand the information provided. The belief is that a red herring will not work on a test taker who fully comprehends the information. For example, read and answer the question below:

Sample

Criminals are people who violate ________________.

a) Penal Code 62
b) Civil procedure
c) Martial law
d) Criminal laws

The correct answer choice is d) Criminal laws. The other answer choices are red herrings designed to distract the inattentive test taker by "sounding" right or formal. While choices a) and c) may be partially correct, breaking a specific penal code (criminal) or martial (civilian-imposed military) law may be a crime, neither is the *best* answer choice.

Be sure to read the question for context and tone, and determine what it is asking. The preceding question asked for a general definition and used verbiage from the question as part of the correct answer. While a criminal might violate a *specific* penal code or martial law, generally, violations can be of *any* criminal law. Because criminals are guilty of crimes and *all* criminal laws involve or pertain to crime, choice d) is the *best* answer.

The following tips assume you have a basic understanding of test taking: how to follow test proctor instructions, properly record answers, make sure the answer for the right question is recorded, and review an answer sheet before submitting it. If you do nothing else to prepare, learn these five quick tips. They will help you focus your efforts and use your time wisely.

- Develop a Time Strategy
    - The examination is 2.5 hours, or 150 minutes, long. If divided equally over the exam, you should have approximately one minute and thirty seconds to answer each question. Pay attention to the time. Note the start and end time

for each section prior to beginning. Make a goal to complete each question in one minute or less. One minute seems like a short amount of time, but it is deceiving. You will likely complete most questions in less than 30 seconds. Develop your strategy such that you finish the easier questions quickly to allow more time to spend on the difficult questions.

  - Don't spend too much time on difficult questions. Mark them, skip them and come back when you have time.

- Focus on the Question

  - Read the question carefully. Do not skim. Words sometimes change meaning based on context. Context is the part of a communication that comes before or after a specific word or passage, and provides clarity or meaning. Make sure you read and understand the question before selecting an answer. Read the following sentences:

    - The police **arrested** Chad when he was 18 years old.

    - Although Chad is 32 years old, his emotional development **arrested** when he was 18 years old.

    Even though the word **arrested** is used in both sentences, it has different meanings, depending on the context.

  - Try to think of an answer before looking at the choices. This can prevent diversions created by "red herrings" or other distractions.

- Correct is Not Always Best

  - Several answers could be *correct*, or close to correct, but you must choose the ***best*** answer choice.

  - Avoid the red herring—the answer choice that is close to the correct answer but is merely a distraction.

- Use the Process of Elimination

  - Eliminate answer choices you know are incorrect. Choose your answer from the remaining choices.

  - For "All of the Above" and "None of the Above" answer choices, look for answer choices that include elements that break the "All" or "None" rule, such as a true element in a group of false elements or vice versa. If one element does not belong with the rest of the group's elements, then the answer cannot be *all*, or *none*, of the above.
  - Reread the question and remaining answers and select an answer choice.

- Guessing is an Option
  - There is no penalty for guessing, so if all else fails, guess.
  - Guesswork is still a matter of deduction; eliminate as many choices as possible before making a guess between the remaining answers.

Writing

Written and verbal communications are equally important in law enforcement. Writing accurate, clear, and concise memos, warrants, and police reports ensures the information provided is as the officer intended. Unclear or confusing verbal communication can create misunderstanding and even danger if an officer is attempting to control a volatile situation. The same is true of written work. Imagine the confusion that wordy, incoherent, error-laden communications could create. Inspect the following two passages as an example of how wordiness and grammatical errors can confuse communication:

1. *On Friday, August 17, 2014, about 1530 hours while working as a patrol officer in full uniform in Sector 2 of River City I heard over my car radio that Officer Smith had two people in front of Superior Court with warrants. I arrived at the Superior Court and met with Officer Smith. Officer Smith told me a woman, identified as Jane Johnson, and a man, identified as Ronald Jones, were at the courthouse. Jane and Ronald were at the court for a family hearing.*

   A records check with River City Records and Warrants confirmed Jane had a misdemeanor warrant, and Ronald had a felony warrant, out of River City.

   Jane and Ronald were arrested without incident to answer for the warrant.

2. *On Friday, August 17, 2014, about 1530 hours I contacted Jane Johnson and Ronald Jones in front of the River City Superior Court. Jane and Ronald were at the court for a family hearing. I had information both parties had active warrants for their arrest.*

   A records check with River City Records and Warrants confirmed Jane had an active misdemeanor warrant for her arrest and Ronald had an active felony warrant for his arrest, both issued by River City.

   I arrested Jane and Ronald without incident to answer for their warrants.

Isn't it much easier to understand passage number two? Are the sentences clear, concise, grammatically correct, and contain all the necessary information? On the other hand, does passage number one seem wordy and filled with grammatical errors? Is it clear or confusing? Unclear reports of search warrants could lead to poor investigations, arrests, and prosecutions, ultimately resulting in the release of a criminal.

Spelling

Spell check and auto correct have made lazy spellers of some of us. Can you remember the last time you spelled a word without the aid of an electronic device? So, why is spelling important in law enforcement? Well, much of what officers write is by hand. That's right, with a pen and paper, at least initially. What's more, any notes or other material an officer writes in connection with a crime or criminal investigation is "discoverable." That means the court can compel an officer to turn over his or her notes and communications to the court and lawyers for both sides. Now, no one is perfect, but who wants to be known as the officer who can barely spell? And right or wrong, it could affect said officer's credibility and competence in the eyes of a jury. Many people believe multiple spelling and grammatical errors tend to show a lack of attention to detail and a tendency towards sloppy work; both are detrimental in police work.

Thankfully, for even the most challenged spellers among us, spelling is the easiest part of the examination to study. And while you could relegate yourself to simply repetitively writing random words on a piece of paper like you did after school when you were in trouble with the teacher, there are more focused methods to improve your performance on a multiple-choice spelling test. It can help to learn the following tips, tricks, and rules, to prevent common spelling errors.

Tips and Tricks

- **Homophones**
    - Homophones are words that sound alike, but are spelled differently and hold different meanings, such as break and brake.
    - Example:
        - Officer Brady stepped on the **brake** to stop the car.
        - Officer Brady took a lunch **break** during his shift.
    - Pay attention to context to make the correct word choice.
- **"i" Before "e" Except After "c"**
    - Generally, the letter "i" comes before the letter "e" in a word except when the "i" is preceded by the letter "c."
    - Examples:
        - **Pie**ce
        - Sal**ie**nt
        - **Cei**ling
        - Con**cei**vable

- There are some notable exceptions where the letter "e" comes before the letter "i" such as:
    - "cien" words, like profi**cien**t;
    - plural words ending in "cies," like poli**cies;** and
    - words with an "ay" sound, like **ei**ght, v**ei**n or n**ei**ghbor
- This is a general rule; other less common exceptions also exist.

- **Pluralizing Words**
    - Generally, nouns become plurals by simply adding the letter "s" to the end of the word, such as radio to radio**s**.
    - Notable Exceptions:
        - Pluralize words ending in "ch," "s," "sh," "x," or "z" by adding "es" to the end.
            - Cat**ch** - Catch**es**
            - Pas**s** - Pass**es**
            - Pu**sh** - Push**es**
            - Anne**x** - Annex**es**
            - Blit**z** - Blitz**es**
        - An Exception to the "ch" rule includes words where the "ch" makes a "k" sound. For those words, simply add the letter "s" to the end of the word.
            - Stoma**ch** - Stomach**s**
        - Pluralize words ending in the letter "y" by changing the "y" to "ies."
            - Batter**y** - Batter**ies**
            - Entr**y** - Entr**ies**
        - Pluralize words ending with a consonant plus the letter "f," or single vowel plus the letter "fe," by changing them to "ves."
            - Kni**fe** - Kni**ves**
            - Shel**f** - Shel**ves**

- **Is it a Possessive or a Contraction?**

  - A contraction is a combination of two words that is shortened by using an apostrophe to indicate the missing letter or letters. For instance, cannot is shortened to can't; the apostrophe stands in for the missing letters "n" and "o."

  - A possessive is a word with an apostrophe added to indicate possession. For example, rather than writing "the duty belt that belongs to Pat," write "Pat's duty belt."

  - A notable exception to this rule, and common mistake, is the improper use of the contraction "it's" as a possessive.
    - The contraction for "it is" or "it has" is "it's." For example, "It's dangerous in that area of town at night."
    - The word "its" is possessive and shows ownership of the pronoun "it," such as "the jury reached *its* verdict" or "the suspect's car was badly damaged and *its* license plate was obscured."

- **Adding** "ed" or "ing"

  - The endings "ed" or "ing" added to a regular verb generally signify the verb's tense. For example, the present tense of the verb to question is question. To show it happened in the past, or in past tense, the word question becomes question**ed**. And to refer to an action that is still happening, present participle, question becomes question**ing**. Changing tense when using a verb in communication is called conjugation. A regular verb is one that follows a typical conjugation pattern.

  - There are some exceptions to the general rule for conjugating regular verbs and include the following:

    - *Verbs ending with a silent "e."* Drop the "e" before adding "ed" or "ing."

      - Fak**e** - Fak**ed** - Fak**ing**
      - Ach**e** - Ach**ed** - Ach**ing**

        - *Verbs ending in the letters "ee."* Do not drop the second "e," instead simply add the letter "d" or "ing."
            - Fr**ee** - Fre**ed** - Free**ing**
            - Agr**ee** - Agre**ed** - Agree**ing**
        - *Doubling consonants when adding "ed" or "ing."*
            - When the verb ends with a single vowel, plus a consonant, and the stress is at the *end* of the word, then you need to double the consonant before adding "ed" or "ing." For example, comMIT: commi**t**/commit**ted**/commi**tting** or stop: STO**P**/stop**ped**/stop**ping**.
            - If the stress is not at the end of the word, then you do not need to double the consonant, such as in TARget: target/target**ed**/target**ing** or VISit: visit/visit**ed**/visit**ing.**
        - Verbs that end with the letter "c" must have the letter "k" added to the word before adding "ed" or "ing," as in panic/pan**icked**/panic**king**.

- **Adding** "ly"
    - Generally, adding "ly" to a word creates an adverb, which describes how an action was carried out, or an adjective, which describes a noun or pronoun. Adding "ly" is straightforward.
        - For words ending in a consonant, such as grim, simply add "ly" to the end: grim**ly.**
        - For words that end in "y," such as greedy, replace the letter "y" with "ily": greed**ily.**
        - For words that end with the letters "le" like subtle, replace the letter "e" with the letter "y": subt**ly.**
- **The Letter Q**
    - The letter "q" is almost always followed by the letter "u," such as in **qu**iet or **qu**ery. Exceptions to this rule exist, but the words that fall within the

exception do not generally make an appearance on grammar tests, nor are any likely to be included in the PELLETB.

- **Ful or Fully**
    - Adding the suffix "ful" to a word generally creates an adjective. Adjectives describe a noun or pronoun, such as grateful. In the sentence "Sally was grateful that Officer Smythe arrived before anyone was hurt," the word grateful describes an attribute about Sally.
    - Adding the suffix "fully" to a word generally creates an adverb. Adverbs describe how an action was carried out. In the sentence "Sally gratefully accepted Officer Smythe's help," the word gratefully describes *how* Sally accepted Officer Smythe's help.

Sample questions

Read the following sentences and choose the correct spelling of the missing word.

1. The defendant asked the court to show him _______ in the punishment for his crime.

    a. Leanency
    b. Leniency
    c. Leneincy
    d. Leniencie

2. Deputy Smith found ________ in the inmate's cell.

    a. Contriband
    b. Controband
    c. Contraband
    d. Contreband

3. Evidence that is fleeting or has the ability to fade away over time is said to be of an _________ nature.

    a. Effervescent
    b. Evanecent
    c. Evanescent
    d. Evenescent

4. Officer Jones attempted to _______ the victim's blood loss by applying pressure to the wound.

    a. Mitagate
    b. Mitegate
    c. Mittigate
    d. Mitigate

Answers

1. b. Leniency; 2. c. Contraband; 3. c. Evanescent; 4. d. Mitigate

See Appendix A for commonly misspelled words related to law enforcement.

Vocabulary

Vocabulary is a collection of words used or known in language. Possessing a large vocabulary can help you better understand communications. It can improve the ability to determine context and add clarity to the written or spoken word. Law enforcement vocabulary can be very technical, but it also contains many commonly used words. The academy teaches technical vocabulary used in law enforcement. The vocabulary section of the PELLETB measures ability to understand and appropriately use *common* words. Each question is structured as one sentence with a word underlined. The answer choices list alternative words to replace the underlined word. You must choose the word that most closely matches the meaning of the underlined word.

Developing a large vocabulary takes time and practice; it cannot be drastically expanded overnight. However, studying commonly used words and their synonyms can help. Synonyms are words that share the same or nearly the same meaning as other words. Understanding word roots, prefixes, suffixes, and how they affect words can also help determine the meaning of unfamiliar words based on the word's structure.

Prefixes, Suffixes, and Root Words

- **Root Words**

  - A root word is the base of a word. It comes after a prefix or before a suffix. Root words hold meaning and can stand alone as words. Learning to recognize common root words can help you build your vocabulary and make educated guesses about unfamiliar words. It can also help improve your ability to comprehend communications.

  - These are some examples of common root words, their meanings and uses. For a more comprehensive list, see Appendix C at the end of this guide.

Root	Meaning	Uses
juven	young	**juven**ile, re**juven**ate
mal	bad	**mal**feasance, **mal**evolent, **mal**content
scrib/scribe	write	tran**scribe**, tran**scription**, pre**scribe**

- **Prefixes**

  - Prefixes are sets of letters that are added to the beginning of a word. Adding a prefix to a word can change its meaning. For instance, if you take the root word "jud," which means judge, and add the prefix, "pre", which means before, you can create the word prejudice, which generally means to prejudge. Prefixes cannot stand on their own as words, but they do hold meaning. Learning to recognize common prefixes can help build your vocabulary and make educated guesses about unfamiliar words. It can also help improve your ability to comprehend communications.

- These are some examples of common prefixes, their meanings and uses. For a more comprehensive list, see Appendix C at the end of this guide.

Prefix	Meaning	Uses
contra-	against	**contra**dict, **contra**ry, **contra**vene
mis-	wrong	**mis**take, **mis**interpret, **mis**construe
pre-	before	**pre**existing, **pre**view, **pre**scient

- **Suffixes**

  - Suffixes are the same as prefixes except that suffixes are added to the ends of words rather than the beginning.

  - These are some examples of common suffixes, their meanings and uses. For a more comprehensive list, see Appendix C at the end of this guide.

Suffix	Meaning	Uses
-able	capable of	move**able**, prevent**able,** excit**able**
-cide	kill	patri**cide**, insecti**cide,** homi**cide**
-ology	study	bi**ology**, physi**ology**, soci**ology**

Sample questions

Choose a word from the answer choices that is closest in meaning to the underlined word. *(Questions 1-5).*

1. The suspect did not have any <u>OUTSTANDING</u> warrants.

   a. Inactive
   b. Unsettled
   c. Unconfirmed
   d. Confirmed

2. Because a career in law enforcement can be dangerous, officers should not become <u>COMPLACENT</u>.

   a. Confident

b. Unsafe
c. Self-satisfied
d. Cheerful

3. During her testimony, the witness RECANTED her statement.

    a. Affirmed
    b. Rescinded
    c. Retold
    d. Regretted

4. The jury did not believe the suspect's mother was a CREDIBLE witness.

    a. Trustworthy
    b. Likeable
    c. Suitable
    d. Useful

5. The suspect's account of the incident was full of DISCREPANCIES.

    a. Falsities
    b. Inaccuracies
    c. Deception
    d. Inconsistencies

Answers and Explanations

1. Correct – b. Unsettled means outstanding, due

    Inactive means dormant
    Unconfirmed means unsupported, uncorroborated
    Confirmed means verified

2. Correct – c. Self-satisfied means complacent

    Confident means sure, secure
    Unsafe means not safe, risky
    Cheerful means pleasant, happy

3. Correct – b. Rescinded means recant

Affirmed means maintain as true, confirm
Retold means told over again in a new way
Regretted means felt remorse for

4. Correct – a. Trustworthy means credible

   Likeable means easy to like
   Suitable means appropriate
   Useful means being of use

5. Correct – d. Inconsistencies means discrepancies

   Falsities means falsehoods or lies
   Inaccuracies means errors or mistakes
   Deception means ruse or trick

See Appendix B for a study list of vocabulary words and Appendix C for a list of common prefixes, suffixes, and root words.

Clarity

Writing clearly and concisely helps readers easily understand a message. In law enforcement, the last thing an officer wishes is for lawyers, juries, or the public to have to *guess* what the officer meant in a report or other written communication. Cases have been won and lost based on officer testimony related to a well written or poorly written report. The Clarity subsection of the PELLETB tests only common grammatical mistakes and requires the test taker to identify the most clearly written of two sentences. Avoiding the common grammatical errors listed below can help add clarity to your written communication.

- **Vague or Unclear References**
    - A vague or unclear reference occurs in a sentence or passage when it is unclear to which antecedent noun the pronoun relates. The nouns are antecedent because they come before the pronoun. For example, in the sentence, "Officer Lane gave Assistant District Attorney Poole *his* notes," it is difficult to determine whose notes the officer gave the A.D.A.
    - Apply the following rules to prevent vague or unclear references:
        - Be sure the pronoun only refers to one antecedent noun. Applying this rule to the above sentence would result in the following change, "Officer Lane gave *his* notes to Assistant District Attorney Poole."
        - Do not use a pronoun to refer to an implied idea, but state the idea explicitly. For instance, writing, "The jury reached a verdict in the defendant's case, but *it* took a long time," could lead the reader to wonder if jury deliberation took a long time, or if the process of the trial took a long time. Applying this rule would change the sentence to, "The jury reached a verdict in the defendant's case, but *the trial* took a long time."
- **Misplaced Modifiers**
    - A modifier is a word or phrase that adds detail to a sentence. It relates to the subject of the sentence. When the modifier is poorly placed in relation to the subject and ends up modifying something else, causing confusion, it is called a misplaced modifier. For example, the sentence "During the trial, the Assistant District Attorney presented the jury with the gruesome victim's photos," can be confusing. Which did the writer mean was gruesome, the

photos or the victim?

  - To prevent misplaced modifiers, keep them as closely as possible to the thing they are modifying. Applying this rule to the above sentence results in the following change, "During the trial, the Assistant District Attorney presented the jury with gruesome photos of the victim."

- **Sentence Fragments**

  - A sentence fragment occurs when a group of words is followed by a period, or preceded by a semicolon and followed by a period, but do not form a complete sentence or thought. The following is an example of a sentence fragment. "Judge Kimball left the bench; tired of presiding over cases involving the same criminals in his courtroom."

  - Be sure each sentence contains a complete thought before adding a period or semicolon and period. Applying this rule changes the preceding sentence to the following, "Judge Kimball left the bench; he was tired of presiding over cases involving the same criminals in his courtroom."

- **Run on Sentences**

  - A run on sentence is two or more complete sentences not separated by appropriate punctuation, such as a comma, period, or semicolon. For example, the following is a run on sentence: "Jack shot his friend Mark over a pool game Jack was mad because he thought Mark was cheating."

  - Be sure to separate each complete thought with proper punctuation. Applying this rule changes the preceding sentence to the following: "Jack shot his friend Mark over a pool game. Jack was mad because he thought Mark was cheating."

Sample questions

In each example, choose the more clearly written sentence:

1.

   a. Jane broke into the house intending to steal items to exchange for drugs she activated the alarm and ran away.
   b. Jane broke into the house intending to steal items to exchange for drugs. She activated the alarm and ran away.

2.

   a. John said he and Frank were fighting when he was shot.
   b. John said he and Frank were fighting when Frank was shot.

3.

   a. During police contacts, failure to follow directions is often the cause of officer uses of force.
   b. During police contacts, failure to follow directions often is the cause of officer uses of force.

4.

   a. The suspect robbed an elderly woman and then fled the scene in a red sedan heading northbound on 8th Avenue.
   b. The suspect robbed an elderly woman and then fled the scene in a red sedan. Heading northbound on 8th Avenue.

Answers and Explanations

1. Choice b is correct. Choice a is incorrect because it is a run on sentence.

2. Choice b is correct. Choice a is incorrect because it contains a vague reference.

3. Choice a is correct. Choice b is incorrect because it has a misplaced modifier.

4. Choice a is correct. Choice b is incorrect because it contains a sentence fragment.

Reading Comprehension

In the land of movies and television, law enforcement officers are rarely shown reading. Dirty Harry, John McClane, Horatio Cane, or Andy Sipowicz would be hard-pressed to pick up the penal code, case notes, or even a newspaper! But, in the real world where shooting up the entire downtown area, costing the city and county millions of dollars in repair costs and civil suits, and turning your back on suspects to don sunglasses can get you fired, sued, or hurt, reading is a huge part of the job.

Law enforcement officers spend a considerable amount of time reading reports, case law, statutes, subpoenas, warrants, investigative notes, memos and policy changes, news reports affecting the community served and policing at large, and much more. Understanding what you read is paramount because it may dictate how you can do the job.

Misunderstanding what you read could cost you your job. Reading comprehension is one of the most important aspects of law enforcement. The PELLETB tests applicants' reading comprehension abilities by presenting a passage for the applicant to read, then asking several questions about the passage's content. The following information provides tips and tricks to improve your skills and navigate the reading comprehension section of the exam.

Reading for Understanding

Reading for understanding is different from reading for entertainment. Rather than simply skimming a passage for generalized information, reading for understanding requires the reader to dig more deeply into the text, make inferences and connections, and evaluate and interpret ideas and information. However, an integral part of reading comprehension is answering questions about the information. To be proficient at comprehension, readers must master several tasks while reading a particular passage:

- **Differentiate fact from opinion**. Many readers cannot tell the difference between fact and opinion. Contrary to popular belief, fact and opinion are not opposites; instead, they are differing types of statements.
    - A fact is a statement that can be proven by direct or objective evidence. It is also a reason juries are called the "finders of fact" because they use the evidence presented to prove a statement.
    - On the other hand, an opinion, though it may be based in fact, is a statement established using belief or judgment and cannot be objectively proven true

or false. Opinions are not necessarily wrong; they simply are not fact.

- **Distinguish between what is important and what is simply interesting.** When determining what is important in a passage, think about the main point and tone. What is the author trying to say? What is the main point?
    - Information that tends to strengthen or weaken the main point is important.
    - Information that does not strengthen or weaken the main point is simply interesting.
- **Determine cause and effect relationships.** Determine if there is a cause and effect relationship between pieces of information contained in the passage. Determining cause and effect relationships is important in comprehension as well as establishing potential outcomes.
    - Look for words that show causal relationships, such as because, since, therefore, thus, and so.
- **Compare and contrast ideas and information.** Connecting words often indicate transition within a passage. Understanding transitions can help keep you on track with the author's main point, rather than confused by opposing points of view in the passage.
    - Look for words that show a shift in the author's position, such as however, but, rather, in contrast, and although.
- **Draw conclusions.** Law enforcement officers regularly make inferences, draw conclusions, and make determinations based on information presented. After reading the passage, ask yourself:
    - What judgments can be made based on the information provided?
    - What evidence included in the passage supports that judgment?
    - Are there other interpretations that can be made using the provided information and evidence?
- **Summarize.** Law enforcement officers often summarize in conversations. To ensure understanding, officers often repeat, in their own words, information a victim or suspect provided. The victim or suspect generally confirms or adjusts the restated information.

   - After reading, take the information that is most important to the author and restate in it your own words.

Deductive vs Inductive Reasoning

There are two main ways to draw conclusions through reasoning—using deduction or induction.

Deductive Reasoning

Deductive reasoning questions test the ability to draw conclusions about a particular point from a general principle. This is also known as the "top down" approach. Reasoning in this manner usually starts with a general statement or hypothesis, and is worked through to a conclusion based on the evidence. Questions that require deductive reasoning follow hard and fast logic rules based on the information provided. The following is an example of an appropriate deduction:

> The court ordered John to be at the courthouse when it opens.
> The courthouse opens at 8:00AM.
>
> Thus, John is required to be at the courthouse at 8:00AM.

Inductive Reasoning

Inductive reasoning questions test the ability to draw conclusions leading to a large principle from a specific point. Inductive reasoning is also called the "bottom up" approach and works the opposite of deductive reasoning. Reasoning in this manner usually starts with an observation or question, and is worked through to a hypothesis by examining related issues. Questions that require inductive reasoning use a more exploratory approach than deduction. The following is an example of appropriate inductive reasoning:

> John should be at the courthouse at 8:00AM because:
> The court ordered John to be at the courthouse when it opens.
> The courthouse is a city building.
> Most city office buildings and facilities open around 8:00AM.

Question Types

Reading comprehension tests generally utilize seven basic question types.

1. **What's the main point?** These questions ask you to identify the author's thesis or hypothesis. A question stem relating to this question type might ask, "The passage was primarily concerned with which of the following?" Check the thesis statement or conclusion for the answer to these types of questions.

2. **What's the supporting idea?** These questions generally ask you to locate specific information. A question stem relating to this question type might ask, "The passage mentions each of the following EXCEPT..." You may need to reread the passage to find the answer. You might look for keywords in the answer choices to help steer you in the right direction.

3. **Drawing inferences**. Questions that require you to draw inferences often ask, "The passage implies which of the following?" The answer choices generally will closely imitate the text of the passage and rely upon specific facts provided.

4. **What's the tone?** These questions ask you to identify the author's attitude. Question stems generally ask, "The author's tone is best described as..."

5. **Apply the theme to other circumstances**. Questions requiring you to apply information from the passage to a similar situation often take the following form: "The author would most likely agree with which of the following?" There is no down and dirty trick to tackle these question types. The key is identifying the heart of the passage and relating it to similar answer choices.

6. **Logical reasoning.** This question style is the reverse of the "Application" question style. Logical reasoning questions ask you to take information from *outside* the passage and apply it to the passage to make determinations. An example of a logical reasoning question might be, "Which of the following, if true, would most weaken the main point of the second paragraph?" Like application style questions, there is no down and dirty trick to tackle logical reasoning question types. The key is identifying the heart of the passage and relating it to similar answer choices.

7. **Relating different ideas**. These questions require you to determine the relationship between different ideas or parts of the passage. Questions are framed in a variety of ways, but might ask how two paragraphs relate to one another, or how an idea in one sentence contrasts with an idea later in the passage.

Quick Tips

Remember these three quick and easy tips for answering reading comprehension questions:

1. **Read the passage carefully**. Do not skim the passage. Read it two or three times to ensure you understand what the passage is communicating. Remember, this section is examining comprehension. Reading too quickly can cause you to miss important information.

2. **Do not read the question stem and or answer choices first**. This can distract you from the main point of the passage and you may fall prey to a red herring answer choice if you answer the question prematurely and without full understanding.

3. **Do not use outside knowledge.** Remember, the answer is located within the passage.

Example Passage and Question Stem

Once an anomaly, nontraditional work hours are becoming a national norm. Many employees currently work night shifts, swing shifts, weekends, and holidays. Nevertheless, they tend to work only five days of the week for about eight hours a day, sometimes during hours when other people are at home. Law enforcement officers and other first responders also participate in shift work; however, the average length of a single shift ranges from 12 to 24 hours rather than eight hours, and shifts run multiple days in a row. First responders work long shifts, partially due to staffing issues and partly because of the nature of the work, as emergencies can happen at any time.

Work as a first responder is a 365-day-a-year, seven-day-a-week, 24-hour-a-day proposition. There are no days when the jails, hospitals, and fire departments are closed for the holiday. As a result, agencies must at all times staff their respective facilities to accommodate the event of any emergency. In law enforcement particularly, staffing cuts due to state and county budget shortfalls have rendered departments short-staffed. Insufficient staffing in jails and on patrol creates serious security and safety issues. Thus, to address the problem, many agencies require employees to work mandatory overtime shifts in addition to their normally assigned shifts. While mandatory overtime temporarily corrects staffing shortages, it adds more hours, and days, to the officers' workweek. Law enforcement officers currently work more hours per day than most people, with less time in between shifts for adequate sleep, nourishment, and time with family or friends. The result is that officers are more sleep-deprived, malnourished, and more prone to illness and injury. Recent studies indicate that officer-involved traffic accidents due to sleep deprivation have also increased. Moreover, studies show that shifts lasting longer than 12 hours per day, for more than three days in a row, exacerbate the issue.

On the other hand, agencies that limit shift work to 10-12 hours per day for three to four days, then allow for three days off duty, have experienced a decrease in problems related to officer sleepiness and nutritional health. Officers working 10-hour shifts report more energy and better sleeping and eating habits. Because officer safety on and off duty is important, many agencies are exploring options for shorter shift formats that do not affect staffing levels.

Question #1: What is the best title for this passage?

a) Long Work Hours for First Responders Cause Sleepiness and Malnutrition
b) Staffing Shortages Lead to Unhealthy Cops
c) Shift Work is a National Norm
d) First Responders Work 365 days a year, 24/7

Question #2: What is the main purpose of the passage?

a) To support working more overtime
b) To draw attention to safety issues in law enforcement
c) To illustrate the relationship between budget cuts and officer safety issues
d) To support shorter shifts for officers

Answers

Question #1: a) This answer choice best captures the main idea of the passage. The other options are supporting ideas or points.

Question #2: d) is correct. Option a) is the opposite of the main purpose. Options b) and c) are supporting ideas.

Reasoning

The reasoning section of the PELLETB measures applicants' ability to relate various pieces of information to one another. Generally, the test examines ordering, grouping, and pattern recognition abilities. Reasoning tests can be intimidating at first, but when armed with a few tricks and some practice, anyone can be successful.

Logical vs Verbal Reasoning

Verbal Reasoning

Verbal reasoning generally applies to the ability to analyze and evaluate written materials and identify relationships between words and concepts. Answering reading comprehension questions is an example of verbal reasoning.

Logical Reasoning

Logical reasoning is similar, but focuses more on analyzing, evaluating, and creating *hypotheses* based on the information given. Logical reasoning tests can be verbal or numerical, but most often rely on numbers and symbols. The PELLETB Reasoning section is a mixture of logic- and verbal-based questions and prompts.

Demystifying Word, Letter, and Number Sequences

Logic tests can be intimidating because few words, and a sea of numbers and blank spaces, confront test takers. The questions appear to require test takers to make what seem like outlandish deductions. Applicants without any background in logic testing may feel as though they've been asked, "You are given a quarter, nickel, dime, and penny; how hot is the sun if it's raining in July?"

The truth is, logic questions are no different from any other reasoning question you've previously faced and crushed. The tricks you've already learned apply, one of which is to look to the question for clues to the answer. For example, answer the following question:

Complete the following sequence.

1, 1, 2, 3, 5, 8, ____

a) 9
b) 11
c) 13
d) 15

The answer is c) 13. If you look at the sequence, you'll notice each number is added to the next number in the sequence to create the following number: **1**+1=**2**, 1+2=**3**, 2+3=**5**, 3+5=**8**, 5+8=**13**. Now that wasn't so bad, was it?

Word, letter, and number sequences all follow similar rules. See below for some tricks to help you master logical reasoning questions.

- **When confronted with numbers, expect to do a little math**. If asked to complete a sequence of numbers, like in the example above, first check to see how the numbers relate to each other mathematically. Start with the easy stuff like addition, subtraction, multiplication, and division.

- **Word sequences may also use some math**. Sometimes a word sequence is based on the numerical position of letters in the alphabet, like a=1 and z=26. Word sequences might also be based on the words' first or last letters in relationship to each other, for example B**a**nana, *A***p**ple, *P***l**um, *L***e**mon. Each item is a type of fruit *and* each successive fruit name begins with the second letter of the preceding fruit's name. The next choice would be a fruit that begins with the letter "e," like Elderberry.

- **One of these things is not like the other**. In grouping questions, look for the odd item in the group. For example, if presented with the following items— bed, hammock, gurney, chair—chair is the odd item in the group because it's the only item used primarily for sitting.

- **Don't be afraid to draw**. When confronted with questions requiring you to order information, make a chart. Use a chart to answer the following question:

  Sarah arrived home at 9:00PM and found her home burglarized. She told the police she left for work at 8:00AM and stopped for dinner after work with some friends. Her husband Joseph was home until 7:00PM because he works the night shift. What time did the burglary occur?

  a) between 8:00AM and 9:00PM
  b) between 7:00PM and 9:00PM
  c) Not enough information

8:00AM Sarah leaves--------------7:00PM Joseph leaves----------------9:00PM Sarah returns

The Answer is b). The house was empty between 7:00PM and 9:00 PM. The burglary likely happened during that time.

CLOZE

What's a CLOZE?

The CLOZE test measures reading comprehension by testing how easy it is for a target audience to read and understand a particular passage. It also measures vocabulary and knowledge of the subject on which the passage is based. Test takers are provided a passage to read. The first and last sentences remain intact and then every seventh word in the passage is deleted. The test requires applicants to provide missing words using context, deduction, and reasoning in order to show that they understand the passage. In many cases, more than one word may fit in a blank space and be considered a correct answer. However, all answers must fit the word length indicated in the passage.

Studying for the CLOZE section of the PELLETB is probably the most difficult for most people. The following chapter can help you develop a strategy for tackling the CLOZE.

Playing Hangman

Have you ever played the game Hangman? As part of the game, your opponent draws a stick figure picture of the gallows above a set of dashes, which correspond to letters and words your opponent is thinking. You can guess any letter in an attempt to fill in the blank dashes with correct letters that make up the missing word. Correct guesses give clues to the missing word or phrase. Incorrect guesses result in pieces of a stick man being added to the gallows. The goal is to guess the word before the stick figured man is completely drawn.

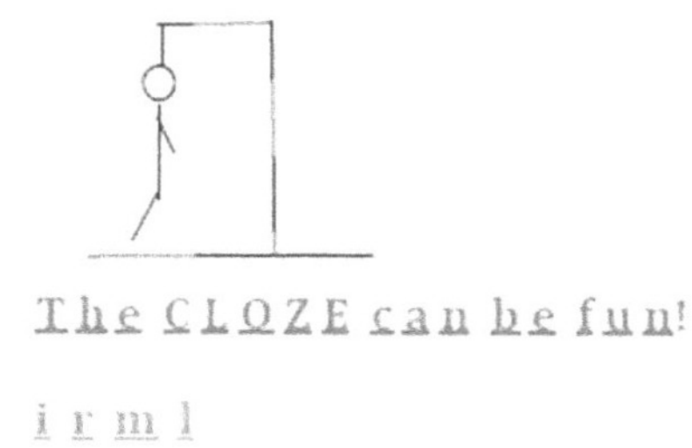

As a kid, playing Hangman was a fun way for friends to challenge each other mentally. The CLOZE test is like a game of Hangman for adults. It has blank lines and clues and challenges your mental grit. Take a look at the following tips to help you succeed on the CLOZE.

- **Look for hints in the writing**.
  - Use context clues. Look for definitions in the passage.
  - Look for meaning or definitions inside quotes or dashes.
  - Sometimes the passage's text provides definitions of unknown words.
- **Read the sentences before and after the missing word very carefully**. The preceding and following sentences often hold clues.
- **Look for words that suggest similarities, like:**
  - same, same as, similarly, also
- **Look for words that suggest opposites, like**:
  - however, on the other hand, but, although, conversely
- **Guess the meaning of sentences or words based on your own knowledge**. This is one place on the PELLETB where your own outside knowledge can be beneficial.
- **Skim or scan the reading**. Before you begin answering questions, read the entire passage for context. You'd be surprised what your brain will "see."

- **Look for repetition.** If you see a noun repeated throughout the passage, that word is usually part of the main idea.
- **Pay attention to tense**. Make note of past, present, and future tense, and make sure the answers use the same tense as the passage.
- **Pay attention to singular or plural.** Make a note of whether preceding and successive words are singular or plural and make sure your answers match.

Sample CLOZE Passage

A job in law enforcement involves much more than just arresting criminals. Officers must have good communication skills. _ _ _ _ also must have the ability to _ _ _ _ _ clear, accurate reports and to understand _ _ _ _ _ _ _ materials. Anyone wishing to become a _ _ _ enforcement officer should work on improving _ _ _ _ _ reading and writing skills prior to _ _ _ _ _ _ _ _ for the job. Brushing up on _ _ _ _ _ _ _ grammar, vocabulary, and spelling is a _ _ _ _ place to start. In addition, applicants _ _ _ _ _ _ also work on understanding context, which _ _ essential. Context is the setting of _ communication. The setting is created by _ _ _ _ _ that come immediately before or after _ given word or passage, which provide _ _ _ _ _ _ _.

Because the PELLETB is designed to _ _ _ _ a very specific group of people, _ _ _ _ _ _ _ _ _ _ should study reading comprehension and vocabulary _ _ _ _ _ _ _ to the law. Study guides focused _ _ the format of the PELLETB can _ _ _ _ applicants prepare for the exam. The more prepared an applicant is, the more likely he or she will be successful.

Answers

1. They/Cops
2. write
3. written
4. law
5. their
6. applying
7. English/Written
8. good
9. should
10. is
11. a
12. words
13. a
14. clarity/context
15. test
16. applicants
17. related
18. on
19. help

Practice Exam One

Timed: 2.5 hours

Writing

The writing test is a 45-question multiple-choice examination measuring three aspects of good writing: clarity, vocabulary, and spelling. Since this is a practice exam, feel free to mark your answers in the book. Remember, on test day, all answers must be marked on the answer sheet.

Clarity

In the following sentence pairs, identify the sentence that is most clearly written, by marking the corresponding letter of the sentence choice.

1.
   a. Julie was happy to get back to her life after the trial she felt she received justice.
   b. Julie was happy to get back to her life after the trial. She felt she received justice.

2.
   a. Marge told Ruth that Marge's supervisor wanted to speak with Ruth.
   b. Marge told Ruth that her supervisor wanted to speak with her.

3.
   a. Kelly did not see the cyclist riding in her blind spot and she hit him with her car as she made the right turn.
   b. Kelly did not see the cyclist riding in her blind spot and she hit him with her car. As she made the right turn.

4.
   a. Officers who train rarely are caught off guard.
   b. Officers who train are rarely caught off guard.

5.
   a. The defendant was angry at the sentence he received. He antagonized the judge out of frustration.
   b. The defendant was angry at the sentence he received he antagonized the judge out of frustration.

6.

a. Police officers who keep up to date with changing laws, policies, and community priorities tend to be more successful than those who do not, unless they are assigned to special covert details that have little contact with ordinary citizens.
b. Police officers who keep up to date with changing laws, policies, and community priorities tend to be more successful. Than those who do not unless they are assigned to special covert details that have little contact with ordinary citizens.

7.

a. Jake and Ronald were playing cards when Ronald shot Jake. In the leg.
b. Jake and Ronald were playing cards when Ronald shot Jake in the leg.

8.

a. Community leaders and law enforcement officers often work together toward common goals. Proactive problem solving and preventing social discord are two such goals.
b. Community leaders and law enforcement officers often work together toward common goals proactive problem solving and preventing social discord are two such goals.

9.

a. Detective Sherman almost got convictions for every felony arrest he ever made.
b. Detective Sherman got convictions for almost every arrest he ever made.

10.

a. Family law courtrooms are among the most dangerous because emotions run high when dealing with family issues.
b. Family law courtrooms are among the most dangerous because emotions run high. When dealing with family issues.

11.

a. Kyle wanted to sing, dance, and act; it's what made him happy.
b. Kyle wanted to sing, dance, and act; participating in the arts is what made him happy.

12.

a. Peaceful protests are part of the fabric of America. Protests are only illegal when they become unlawful assemblies or riots.
b. Peaceful protests are part of the fabric of America protests are only illegal when they become unlawful assemblies or riots.

13.

a. While happily at work downtown, Mary's house was burglarized.
b. While Mary was happily at work downtown, her house was burglarized.

14.

a. Fingerprints were collected on print cards by officers.
b. Fingerprints were collected by officers on print cards.

15.

a. Fran was very afraid, but she kept her fear hidden.
b. Fran was very afraid, but she kept it hidden.

Vocabulary

Choose a word from the answer choices that is closest in meaning to the underlined word. *(Questions 16-22)*

16. Kenneth felt <u>APATHETIC</u> in his employment so he decided to quit his job and go to law school.

    a. motivation
    b. dissatisfied
    c. indifferent
    d. unsure

17. Hank was drunk and <u>BELLIGERENT</u> because his wife left him.

    a. hostile
    b. sad
    c. angry
    d. loud

18. After years of daily observing people in the worst situations of their lives, Austin's behavior became <u>CALLOUS.</u>

    a. mean
    b. insensitive
    c. annoyed
    d. empathetic

19. Lucy was nervous, but she did not want to <u>HINDER</u> her daughter's dream of becoming a police officer.

    a. encourage
    b. expedite
    c. crush
    d. impede

20. Clyde was <u>LUCID</u> when he told the paramedics who shot him.

    a. confused
    b. rational
    c. emotional
    d. incomprehensible

21. Larry thought his neighbor, John, was <u>PILFERING</u> Larry's morning newspaper, so he put poison in John's koi pond.

    a. stealing
    b. borrowing
    c. moving
    d. returning

22. Sarah had an <u>INCONSPICUOUS</u> scar on her arm from a car accident several years earlier.

    a. large
    b. prominent
    c. unnoticeable
    d. small

Choose a word from the answer choices that is most opposite the underlined word. *(Questions 23-25)*

23. After working 8, 12-hour shifts in a row, Deputy Nyugen developed a PERSISTENT cough.

    a. lasting
    b. intermittent
    c. unrelenting
    d. harsh

24. Case law sometimes SUPERSEDES legislated law and statutes.

    a. supports
    b. overrides
    c. lowers
    d. boosts

25. If used successfully, the "heat of passion" defense can MITIGATE murder to manslaughter.

    a. lessen
    b. bolster
    c. extend
    d. change

Questions 26-28 provide two words choices in order to complete the sentences below. Choose the word that makes the most sense based on the context of the sentence.

26. The tactical commander outlined the ____________ of action for the SWAT team.

    a. coarse
    b. course

27. The nightly news reported that the police apprehended the ____________ killer who had been tormenting River City residents.

    a. cereal
    b. serial

28. Increased penalties for criminal activity in River City did not appear to have an ____________ on the occurrence of crime.

    a. effect
    b. affect

Choose the best synonym for the underlined word from the answer choices below. *(Questions 29-30)*

29. Deputy Wilson worked very hard to <u>HONE</u> her skills as an officer.

    a. build
    b. sharpen
    c. steady
    d. improve

30. Each year, many laws and statutes are <u>REPEALED</u>.

    a. revoked
    b. updated
    c. added
    d. reworded

Spelling

Read the following sentences and choose the correct spelling of the missing word.

31. The jury foreman turned ____________ the defendant when he read the verdict.

    a. tward
    b. toword
    c. toward
    d. tword

32. The District Attorney _____________ dropped off the case files this morning.

    a. leason
    b. liason
    c. laison
    d. liaison

33. The legislature ______________ the law when it was ruled unconstitutional.

    a. resinded
    b. recinded
    c. rescinded
    d. resended

34. Even the defendant was ____________ when the jury returned a not guilty verdict.

    a. surprised
    b. suprised
    c. supprised
    d. surprized

35. Officer Jones had a ______________ to speak loudly, which often upset people.

    a. tendancy
    b. tendency
    c. tendencie
    d. tendincy

36. Officer uses of force are ___________ and appropriate actions when suspects fail to comply, and escalate police contacts in a manner that jeopardizes safety.

    a. necessary
    b. nesisarry
    c. necassery
    d. necissary

37. John Smith told the court he did not recognize the authority of the _____________ and was filing a lawsuit against it to reclaim money owed him as a right of birth.

    a. goverment
    b. govermant
    c. govirnment
    d. government

38. Pursuant to federal and state laws, all jails and prisons make reasonable ______________ for inmates suffering from various disabilities, to ensure they have the same or comparable access as inmates who do not suffer from a disability.

    a. acomodations
    b. accommodations
    c. accommadations
    d. accomodations

39. Jane filed a restraining order against her ex-boyfriend because he was _____________ her at work.

    a. harassing
    b. harrassing
    c. harasing
    d. herassing

40. Bystanders were ________ upset after witnessing such a horrific accident.

    a. noticably
    b. noticibly
    c. noticeably
    d. noticeabally

41. Jason was arrested because he was in _____________ of stolen property.

    a. posession
    b. possesion
    c. possetion
    d. possession

42. River City Police Department found itself under _____________ after an officer, who was chasing a dangerous criminal, crashed his patrol car into a storefront during business hours.

    a. siege
    b. seige
    c. seege
    d. seage

43. At his sentencing, Jim _____________ apologized for his role in the home invasion robbery.

    a. publicly
    b. publicallie
    c. publicaly
    d. publicely

44. People who are under the influence of certain drugs can become stronger, unpredictable, and more _______________ than an average person.

    a. agresive
    b. aggresive
    c. aggressive
    d. agressive

45. Marge worked long hours as a court reporter and often suffered headaches from extended exposure to _________________ lighting.

    a. floresent
    b. florescint
    c. flourescent
    d. fluorescent

Reading Comprehension

The reading comprehension test measures ability to read and understand various written materials. Read each paragraph or passage and choose the response that best answers the question. All questions are self-contained and use only information provided in the passage that precedes them.

Questions 46-52

When people think critically, they examine, evaluate, and synthesize information they've gathered in order to arrive at a logical conclusion. Critical thinking can be accomplished at a simple or more probing level, depending on whether a cursory or more thoughtful conclusion is desired. At its most basic level, critical thinking is an activity necessary for people to function properly in society. Every day, without thought, most people engage in simple critical thinking exercises as they interact with one another. They observe, analyze, and assess clues and information around them, in order to understand others' behavior and to make decisions about how to respond appropriately. When used purposefully, critical thinking can help gain a much greater understanding of the gathered information. However, many people do not wish to move beyond this basic, instinctual level when deep critical thinking is not imperative. They do not wish to gain deeper understanding of a person or issue even though it may be as simple as asking, "why?"

Intensive critical thinking is employed most often in academic settings. Teachers challenge students to apply a higher order of thinking skills, to avoid oversimplification, to be objective, and always to ask the next question such as, "why," "what," or "what if," to make reasoned judgments. Critical thinking in academia generally requires a supposition, facts and information, and the ability to infer a logical conclusion from one or more assertions. In academia, critical thinking can be either relegated to mere theoretical dialogue, or applied to an actual problem in order to generate improved conditions.

Since the 1970's, critical thinking has also been used in police work. It is vital, purposeful, and systematic. Police must analyze crimes and criminal activity, establish facts, and determine what information remains unknown. Police investigators analyze patterns and evidence to determine how and why criminal activity was committed and who committed the crime. They ask the questions, "What's missing?" "What are the benefits of the crime?" "Who benefitted?" "Was the crime planned or opportunistic?" Each question probes deeper into the issue and helps investigators uncover clues to reconstruct other people's reasoning. Critical thinking in police work questions the known facts of a case in such a way that investigators are able to understand criminal actions, and those who commit them, more accurately. It can help investigators understand a perpetrator's state of mind, determine what the perpetrator was thinking, how he or she was thinking, as well as to establish the investigator's opinion of what, how, and why a particular event occurred.

Recently, critical thinking has become even more vital to law enforcement because criminals continue to become more savvy. As technology has evolved, so has crime sophistication. Criminals have to work smarter not to be apprehended, thus detectives work smarter by studying, evaluating, and assessing evidence to successfully investigate and prosecute criminals.

46. The tone of the author can be best described as:

    a) Objective
    b) Argumentative
    c) Passionate
    d) Empathetic

47. As used in paragraph 1, what is the best synonym for *imperative*:

    a) Absolutely necessary
    b) Very important
    c) Completely unnecessary
    d) Avoidable

48. According to the passage, it can be inferred that the author believes which of the following:

    I. Critical thinking is used in many ways.
    II. Critical thinking is only important in academia.
    III. Critical thinking is vital in police work.

    a) III only
    b) II only
    c) II and III only
    d) I and III only

49. Which of the following, if true, weakens the main point of paragraph 3?

    a. People do not use critical thinking in everyday life.
    b. Law enforcement began using critical thinking methods in the 1990's.
    c. Academics do not apply theory to real life situations.
    d. Fewer crimes are successfully investigated and prosecuted since police began using critical thinking methods.

50. As used in paragraph 4, what is the best definition of *savvy*?

    a. Cool
    b. Shrewd
    c. Inexperienced
    d. Dangerous

51. What is the best title for this passage?

    a. The Definition of Critical Thinking
    b. Critical Thinking and Law Enforcement
    c. The Many Applications of Critical Thinking
    d. Critical Thinking: A Survey

52. According to the passage, what is the main reason for the application of critical thinking in police work?

    a. To help investigators understand criminal activity and criminal perpetrators more accurately
    b. To determine how criminal activity was committed and who committed the crime
    c. Because crime sophistication has evolved and thus investigators must also evolve
    d. All of the above
    e. A and B only

Questions 53-57

River City Police Department policy mandates that officers remain in good physical condition while employed with the department. Most officers would gladly comply but commute times, long work hours, and mandatory overtime account for about 15 hours of each officer's day. Officers recently asked River City about developing a wellness program for staff members, sworn staff in particular, including the ability to exercise in one of the many gyms located at various River City Police Department's satellite facilities. The resulting memo from the River City Chief of Police was disseminated to all staff.

Dear Staff,

It gives me great pleasure to work at an agency that is full of hardworking, motivated individuals, sworn and civilians alike, who seek new ways to continue improving themselves in both professional and personal life.

As you are aware, law enforcement is a physical job that requires the men and women who do the job to maintain a high level of physical fitness. I'm confident all of you would like to maintain that high level of physical fitness. I know this is difficult for many who have family obligations, long commutes from your respective homes in the outlying areas, and work copious overtime shifts. These factors have undoubtedly created barriers for you to reach your personal goals and the required baseline goals of this department.

It was recently brought to my attention that a number of you requested permission to exercise at your duty station during your workday, on your meal break, in one of the various gyms we maintain on facility sites, in order to make exercising easier to fit into your daily routine. I, as well as the warriors who work out with me every morning, would love for you to join us. And although I understand your various dilemmas, for reasons of liability, worker's compensation issues, as well as the logistical issues involved in managing meal breaks so an entire duty station is not working out at the same time, I must deny that request. I will, however, work with you in other ways to help you meet your fitness goals.

As of next week, the following policies will take effect under the River City Police Employee Wellness Pledge program:

- We will update our meal program for staff members assigned to duty stations where leaving base during shifts is disallowed. We will no longer provide hamburgers, soda, french fries, bacon, or chips. For those of you who work the night shift and eat breakfast, eggs and hash brown potatoes will still be available. If you would like to purchase a soda or snack during your 12-hour shift, you may do so at the remaining vending machines on-site.

- You may not exercise at any gym during duty hours, even if you are on break. You are welcome to work out before or after your assigned shift at any of our beautiful gyms.
- We will begin a physical fitness club that will meet once a month at one of our facilities for organized workouts. This club is open to the first 30 people who sign up.

Thank you for your diligence to do the job well and to make River City the best police department in the state. I look forward to helping you meet your fitness goals, and to your feedback on this exciting new program.

Keep up the good work!

Sincerely,

Chief J. Hyde

53. What is the main point of the Chief's letter?

    a. Physical fitness is important.
    b. The Chief is willing to help.
    c. The Chief does not want to be responsible for staff who exercise on duty.
    d. It is primarily the responsibility of the employee to figure out how to manage time for workouts.

54. What is the overall tone of the Chief's letter?

    a. Cordial
    b. Angry
    c. Passionate
    d. Sarcastic

55. According to the Chief, what is the main reason he denied the request to work out during work hours?

    a. Staff should be working
    b. Even though staff may be on break, River City is still liable for injuries
    c. Logistics
    d. Both B and C

56. According to the passage, how many hours in a given day does the average River City officer have left to eat, sleep, run errands, and work out after he or she released from duty?

    a. 15
    b. 17
    c. 9
    d. 11

57. What is the best meaning of the word *warrior* as used in paragraph 3?

    a. A person experienced in warfare; a soldier
    b. A person who shows great vigor
    c. A person who fights to work out
    d. Both B and C

Questions 58-60

These days, it is harder than ever for kids to simply "walk away" from a bully. Bullying amongst children and adolescents has evolved beyond taunting a smaller or less popular kid while he or she is at school, to cyber stalking children across city and state lines with the use of common electronic devices. Because of the increasing reach of bullies, among other things, suicides and violent confrontations between youth has risen over the years.

Because of the current scope of bullying, school administrators no longer rely solely on teachers to keep kids safe while at school. Rather, administrators build teams of collaborators that include health care workers, teachers, administration, security staff, and law enforcement personnel to ensure schools remain a safe place for kids to learn. School Resource Officers (SROs) receive training in issues that are unique to youth. Generally, SROs have an office on campus. They are stationed at the school and spend their time dealing with law enforcement issues. They also spend a great deal of time talking to kids about anything that interests them, such as school activities, sports, law enforcement, and life in general. Since SROs talk to kids at particular schools regularly, officers are in a unique position to identify emerging issues and prevent them before they develop into greater problems.

SROs play a large role in managing situations that involve bullying so that *all* involved students and families are heard and respected.

58. According to the passage, why has bullying become so prevalent?

   a. Technological advancement
   b. School Resource Officers on school grounds
   c. Meaner kids
   d. Boredom

59. Which fact, if true, strengthens the author's main point?

   a. More kids are bullied currently than in previous years
   b. The majority of bullying happens over electronics
   c. School Resource Officers are needed on school grounds
   d. Both A and B

60. According to the passage, who is involved in managing bullying at schools?

   a. School Officials
   b. Law Enforcement
   c. Medical Professionals
   d. All of the above

Questions 61-65

With over 22 million staff members and students on college campuses across the nation, campus security has moved to the forefront as an opportunity for security staff to be proactive, educating the college community about campus life and being safe while in a home away from home.

Depending on the size and location of a given school, campus security staffing and scope might be small-scale and cozy or monolithically entrenched in the campus community. Additionally, some campuses employ full-time police agencies while others employ independent contractors or private security companies. Because the nature and scope of each campus security department varies so widely, the level of communication with other security and law enforcement departments also varies. Now is a crucial time, given the recent tragic events on college campuses and the sheer number of people continually on campuses, to begin creating universal standards so that all kids and staff members have the same level of protection regardless of the school where they choose to attend or work.

61. As used in paragraph 1, what is the best definition of the word *monolithically*?

    a. Stonelike
    b. Impenetrable
    c. Massive
    d. Miniscule

62. According to the passage, what types of agencies are employed as campus security?

    a. Security companies
    b. Law enforcement
    c. Contractors
    d. All of the above

63. According to the passage, what is an important issue that needs to be addressed?

    a. Communication between agencies
    b. Size of security agency
    c. Both A and B
    d. None of the above

64. Which of the following, if true, most weakens the argument regarding interagency communication?

    a. Smaller operations have more money to spend on communications
    b. Interoperability between campuses is based on size and scope
    c. Each operation, regardless of size and scope, uses its own dedicated communication system
    d. None of the above

65. Based on the tone of the passage, it can be inferred that the author believes which statement about campus security?

    a. Campus security operations are varied to the point of not functioning properly
    b. Size and scope does not necessarily matter if the operation functions properly
    c. Large campus security operations are more safe
    d. Small campus security operations are more safe

Logical Reasoning

The logical reasoning section measures how well you relate various pieces of information to each other. Information is provided as a group, an ordered series of facts, or sequence of numbers or words. Choose the best answer based on the information provided.

Bonus Questions

In the morning, a team of drug enforcement officers will be serving a search warrant on a house at 3456 Beverly Way in River City. You will accompany them, but need to study the information below and answer the questions in order to include the appropriate information in your report. Questions 66-70 will be based on the following information.

I. There are six houses on the street but none of the street addresses are clearly visible.
II. There are three houses on each side of the street.
III. The team has labeled the houses Adam, Boy, Charles, David, Edward, and Frank.
IV. The houses have differing lot sizes.
V. The houses are colored white, blue, green, yellow, red, and orange.
VI. The largest lot size, David house, is exactly opposite the yellow house.
VII. The smallest lot size is exactly opposite the white house.
VIII. The red house, Edward house, is located directly between Charles and Boy houses.
IX. The green house, Frank house, is exactly opposite Charles house.
X. The white house, Adam house is exactly opposite Edward house.
XI. The blue house, Charles house, has a larger lot size than Frank house but smaller than Boy house and Adam house.

66. Which house has the smallest lot size?

a. Charles house
b. Edward house
c. Frank house
d. None of the above

67. Which house has the second largest lot size?

a. Charles house
b. Edward house
c. Frank house

d. None of the above

68. Which color is the largest house diagonal to the green house?

    a. Yellow
    b. White
    c. Blue
    d. Orange

69. What is the color of the house with the second smallest lot?

    a. Orange
    b. Red
    c. White
    d. Green

70. Which house is diagonal from David House?

    a. Boy
    b. Edward
    c. Charles
    d. Frank

71. Three of the words below are similar and one is different. Choose the word that is different.

    a. Helicopter
    b. Airplane
    c. Blimp
    d. Train

72. If some lawyers are cops and teachers, and some teachers are cops and lawyers, and some cops are lawyers and teachers, which of the following is true?

    a. All cops are teachers
    b. No cops are lawyers
    c. Some people are cops, lawyers, and teachers
    d. Some people are teachers and lawyers only
    e. Both C and D
    f. None of the Above

73. Three of the words below are similar and one is different. Choose the word that is different.

    a. Potato
    b. Strawberry
    c. Onion
    d. Banana

Study the sequence of numbers or letters below and complete the sequence.

74. Ape, Buffalo, Cat, ___

    a. Elephant
    b. Deer
    c. Dove
    d. Giraffe

75. 2, 4, 6, 8, ___, 12.

    a. 9
    b. 10
    c. 7
    d. 5

76. Which word comes next in the series?
    Arrest, Detain, Grants, Jailer, _____

    a. Search
    b. Motion
    c. Handcuff
    d. Prison

CLOZE

Questions 77-116

CLOZE

On this part of the test, fill in each blank with the appropriate word. The words are indicated by blank spaces and dashes within the passage. Each dash represents a letter. The word must be correct, given the context of the passage, and it must have the same number of letters as dashes. All words that meet both criteria are considered correct. More than one word may be appropriate for a given space.

More than 25 years ago, law enforcement first partnered with community leaders in an attempt to bridge the gap between the police and the communities they serve. Law enforcement had long since realized _ _ _ _ _ _ _ _ changes were making it more and _ _ _ _ difficult to do the job without _ _ _ _ _ _ _ _ _ support. Because police could not do _ _ _ job alone, and thus did the _ _ _ poorly in certain communities, community trust _ _ _ _ _ to falter. The creation of community _ _ _ _ _ _ _ _ programs was a way to rebuild _ _ _ community trust as well as reinvigorate _ _ and allow police to do their _ _ _ better. Initial community policing programs were _ _ _ _ _ _ _ _ _ designed to help community members mobilize _ _ _ _ _ _ _ and resources to solve problems, voice _ _ _ _ _ concerns, contribute advice, and take action _ _ address concerns. But, these initial programs _ _ _ _ _ _ to be paternalistic, and while some _ _ _ _ _ _ _ _ _ _ _ showed improvement, the improvement was slow. _ _ other communities, residents and leaders outright _ _ _ _ _ _ _ _ the efforts of the police to _ _ _ _ together.

Over the years, community policing _ _ _ _ _ _ _, moving away from the paternalism of _ _ _ _ _ programs and toward more true collaboration. _ _ _ _ _ _ than simply "voicing opinions," which police _ _ _ _ took under advisement while determining an _ _ _ _ _ _ plan; community members became bonafide stakeholders _ _ _ _ _ _ _ equal control over community priorities and _ _ _ _ _ _ plans. Today, community policing exists as _ collaborative effort between police, and community _ _ _ _ _ _ _ _ _ _ _ _ _ such as, schools, community based organizations, _ _ _ _ _ _ _ _ _ _ _, local government and residents, designed to _ _ _ _ _ _ _ _, prioritize and solve community problems. The _ _ _ _ _ _ _ _ community policing philosophy promotes organizational strategies _ _ _ _ use this collaboration to problem-solve _ _ _ proactively address persistent or emerging public _ _ _ _ _ _ problems such as crime and social _ _ _ _ _ _ _ _. All current community programs must be _ _ _ _ _ on three essential components, collaborative partnerships, _ _ _ _ _ _ _ _ _ _ _ _ _ _ transformation to support said partnerships and _ _ _ _ _ _ _ solving methods, along with a proactive, _ _ _ _ _ _ _ _ examination of identified issues and effective _ _ _ _ _ _ _ _ evaluation. As a result, models of community policing exist in most police agencies across the nation and the communities they serve, crisis situations have decreased in many communities, and the police have a markedly improved relationships with the citizens they serve.

Practice Exam Two

Timed: 2.5 hours

Writing

The writing test is a 45-question multiple-choice examination measuring three aspects of good writing: clarity, vocabulary, and spelling. Since this is a practice exam, feel free to mark your answers in the book. Remember, on test day, all answers must be marked on the answer sheet.

Clarity

In the following sentence pairs, identify the sentence that is most clearly written by marking the corresponding letter of the sentence choice.

1.
   a. The bus driver lost control of the bus while turning a corner. Too fast.
   b. The bus driver lost control of the bus while turning a corner too fast.

2.
   a. Steven saw his stolen car on the way to work.
   b. On the way to work, Steven saw his stolen car.

3.
   a. Jared drank several alcoholic beverages at the party. He crashed into a parked car on the way home and was arrested for DUI.
   b. Jared drank several alcoholic beverages at the party he crashed into a parked car on the way home and was arrested for DUI.

4.
   a. Officer Daryn said he didn't like to drive in pursuits because the fast speeds make you sick.
   b. Officer Daryn said he didn't like to drive in pursuits because the fast speeds make him sick.

5.

a. Generally, most people remain unaware of the judicial system's. Process unless they become a party to an action.
b. Generally, most people remain unaware of the judicial system's process unless they become a party to an action.

6.

a. As the defendant was remanded into custody, the judge lectured him.
b. The judge lectured the defendant as he was remanded into custody.

7.

a. Court clerks are essential members of the court staff they maintain all the court documents and record each word spoken in court while "on the record."
b. Court clerks are essential members of the court staff. They maintain all the court documents and record each word spoken in court while "on the record."

8.

a. Jack called the Sheriff's Office but they didn't return his call.
b. Jack called the Sheriff's Office answering service but the answering service didn't return his call.

9.

a. Greg's neighbor has a dog. That barks all hours of the day and night.
b. Greg's neighbor has a dog that barks all hours of the day and night.

10.

a. Officer Brandt reported the car stolen.
b. The car was reported stolen by Officer Brandt.

11.

a. Community policing is not a new concept it has however recently received a facelift.
b. Community policing is not a new concept. It has however recently received a facelift.

12.

a. Eagerly awaiting time off, Olivia's vacation was just about to start.
b. Eagerly awaiting time off, Olivia was just about to start her vacation.

13.

a. Stoplights are often timed for safety when a driver "jumps" the green, they are usurping the system and the results could be deadly.
b. Stoplights are often timed for safety. When a driver "jumps" the green, they are usurping the system and the results could be deadly.

14.

a. Inmates received lunches in bags from deputies.
b. Inmates received lunches from deputies in bags.

15.

a. Every time Alex turned on the television, they said another city was experiencing unrest.
b. Every time Alex turned on the television, the news reported another city was experiencing unrest.

Vocabulary

Choose a word from the answer choices that is closest in meaning to the underlined word. *(Questions 16-22)*

16. Julian became <u>FRANTIC</u> when he realized his child was missing.

a. frenzied
b. calm
c. frustrated
d. upset

17. Henry only <u>EXACERBATED</u> the problem when he poured water on a grease fire.

a. hurt
b. reduced
c. aggravated
d. excited

18. Deputy Hanes writes reports that tend to be <u>VERBOSE</u>.

    a. concise
    b. clear
    c. confusing
    d. wordy

19. One purpose of community policing is to <u>FOSTER</u> relationships between the police and the communities they serve.

    a. alleviate
    b. create
    c. discourage
    d. promote

20. Case law sometimes <u>SUPERSEDES</u> legislated law and statutes.

    a. supports
    b. overrides
    c. lowers
    d. boosts

21. The jury came to a <u>DUBIOUS</u> conclusion based on the evidence.

    a. clear
    b. questionable
    c. obvious
    d. definite

22. Officers <u>FURTIVELY</u> infiltrated the gang in order to gather intelligence.

    a. stealthily
    b. fraudulently
    c. brazenly
    d. openly

Choose a word from the answer choices that is most opposite the underlined word. *(Questions 23-25)*

23. Judge Singleton <u>ABDICATED</u> her seat on the bench because she was seriously ill.

    a. left
    b. maintained
    c. abandoned
    d. relinquished

24. The jury was admonished and advised that they could not <u>DEVIATE</u> from the instructions.

    a. diverge
    b. depart
    c. sway
    d. remain

25. Toby made his way to the top with <u>GUILE,</u> and swindled thousands of people out of millions of dollars.

    a. duplicity
    b. assistance
    c. honesty
    d. savvy

Questions 26-28 provide two word choices in order to complete the sentences below. Choose the word that makes the most sense based on the context of the sentence.

26. When Tom spoke at the town hall meeting, he intended his words to motivate people to fight for their rights, not to __________ a riot.

    a. incite
    b. insight

27. Mayor Brighton did not __________ whether Tom's speech was protected by the 1st Amendment of the constitution.

    a. know
    b. no

28. Jerry had not eaten in four days and had no money, so he decided to __________ some food to get by.

    a. steel
    b. steal

Choose the best synonym for the underlined word from the answer choices below. *(Questions 29-30)*

29. Some criminals manage to have an <u>AFFABLE</u> demeanor despite the atrocity of their crimes.

    a. warm
    b. friendly
    c. angry
    d. wonderful

30. Sally <u>ALIENATED</u> all of her family and friends when she became addicted to drugs.

    a. angered
    b. estranged
    c. frustrated
    d. united

Spelling

Read the following sentences and choose the correct spelling of the missing word.

31. The relationship of the prosecution and the defense is ______________ by design.

    a. adversarial
    b. advirsarial
    c. advirsareal
    d. adverserial

32. The judge ruled the information was not _______________ to the case and thus inadmissible.

    a. germain
    b. germean
    c. girmain
    d. germane

33. The tension in the courtroom was _______________ as the jury prepared to read the verdict.

    a. palpible
    b. palpable
    c. palpebal
    d. palpabal

34. The judge signed a ___________ in order to compel the company to turn the phone records over to the police.

    a. supena
    b. suppena
    c. subpoena
    d. supeana

35. Judy was ______________ of her son, who suddenly had a lot of money and rarely came home at night.

    a. suspisious
    b. suspisios
    c. suspiscious
    d. suspicious

36. At the scene of a car accident, Officer Dane attempted to _______________ the exchange of information between drivers because they were arguing with each other.

    a. fasilitate
    b. fascilitate
    c. facilitate
    d. facilatate

37. As a victim of a ________________ crime, Mack devoted his time to changing legislation regarding victim's rights.

    a. heinous
    b. hanous
    c. haneous
    d. hienous

38. Mark was an ________________ child who would not listen to his parents and continued to get into trouble.

    a. incorrigable
    b. inccorigable
    c. incorrigeable
    d. incorrigible

39. Officer Sasser knew the importance of attention to detail and never performed her duties in a ______________ manner.

    a. perfunctary
    b. perfunctory
    c. perfunctiry
    d. perfunctery

40. Sovereign citizens are people who belong to a _____________ organization and refuse to recognize the authority of the United States.

    a. seditious
    b. seditiuos
    c. saditious
    d. siditious

41. The president of the neighborhood watch called the police and requested a house be placed under ________________ because its occupants were suspected of drug dealing.

    a. survailance
    b. surveillance
    c. survielance
    d. servielance

42. Stella survived her attack because she was ____________________.

    a. tenacious
    b. tinasious
    c. tenasious
    d. tanancious

43. Ed was arrested for ______________ because he was drunk and sleeping on a park bench at 2 o'clock in the afternoon.

    a. vagrency
    b. vagrincie
    c. vagrincy
    d. vagrancy

44. The suspect was ________________ for four hours before he confessed.

    a. interrogated
    b. interogated
    c. interragated
    d. interagated

45. Four _____________________ witnesses placed Harry at the scene of the crime.

    a. indapendant
    b. independent
    c. independant
    d. indapendent

Reading Comprehension

The reading comprehension test measures ability to read and understand various written materials. Read each paragraph or passage and choose the response that best answers the question. All questions are self-contained and use only information provided in the passage that precedes them.

Questions 46-52

Since the police usually do not have the opportunity to watch a crime as it happens, they must rely on evidence, statements from witnesses and involved parties, and deduction skills to draw conclusions about what actually occurred. Although reliance on information from others is essential, often the information officers receive is inaccurate either because the individual was mistaken in their perception, was biased, or was purposefully deceptive. Police must skillfully sift through all of the information they receive and decide which is accurate and which is not. The officer's decision generally is based on his or her assessment of the information's source, and whether *it* is credible or reliable. There are three main reasons information is unreliable.

The most frequent type of unreliable information is mistaken perception. Mistaken perception happens when otherwise honest and reliable people give information they believe to be true, but is not. Mistaken perception can happen for a number of reasons. For example, during a stressful situation the brain releases adrenaline into the body, causing physiological changes. During periods of extreme stress, blood rushes away from non-essential organs and systems toward the heart. As this happens, people often experience various sensory disturbances, like time anomalies. Often witnesses and involved parties will report that a greater or lesser amount of time passed than actually did. A time anomaly affects an individual's sense of time, which appears to be moving at lightning speed or in slow motion. Sight and sound may also be affected. Witnesses and involved parties experiencing auditory occlusion often describe a temporary loss or lessening of hearing; sounds are muted or unheard. People also experience the feeling of tunnel vision, where peripheral vision is diminished and they can only see what is directly in front of them. People who undergo these physiological changes, even when mild, may have a distorted perception of the incident even though they are telling the truth based on their recollection. Police officers must pay attention to behavior cues that signal an individual may have altered perception due to physiological disturbances.

Another issue with involved party reliability is individual bias. While some people have biases they are aware of, sometimes people have biases they are unaware of for a number of reasons. The bias may stem from accepting another source of information as true without question. In other words, the individual was uncritical of the information received and then passed along to police. People also may have a bias due to a vested interest in a particular view or outcome, and their perception is altered by that interest. Police officers must be diligent in identifying any possible biases during the interview process when establishing witness accuracy and reliability.

Lastly, there are times when people are simply dishonest. The reason for their dishonesty may have nothing to do with the situation at hand. The motivation for the dishonesty may or may not be relevant to the incident, but it is crucial when determining the reliability of the statement itself. If a person is willing to be dishonest to the police, for whatever reason, his or her credibility must also be called into question. Police officers must pay attention to accounts of an incident by witnesses and involved parties for inconsistencies and blatant misinformation.

There are many reasons that accounts of an incident by witnesses and involved parties might be unreliable. It is the officer's duty to use critical thinking, deduction, and logical reasoning to determine what is or is not reliable and why. Police officers have a variety of tools at their disposal in order to determine the accuracy of witness or involved party statements. Corroboration, witness expertise, police officer observations, evidence located at the scene, and the like, can help an officer analyze the information to determine the probable reliability of a statement.

46. What is the main point of this article?

    a. Witnesses are dishonest
    b. Witnesses can be unreliable
    c. Stress can alter witnesses' perception
    d. Biased witnesses are unreliable

47. The passage implies which of the following?

    a. Because witnesses are often unreliable, officers must be diligent in their investigation
    b. Dishonest witnesses are never reliable
    c. Mistaken perception cannot be controlled by the perceiver
    d. Both A and B

48. According to this article, what is the main reason for witness reliability issues?

  a. Dishonesty
  b. Mistaken perception
  c. Bias
  d. All of the above

49. According to the passage, which of the following is true?

  a. People are dishonest for no reason
  b. Some people are unaware of bias they hold
  c. During high stress situations, blood rushes away from non-essential organs to the heart
  d. Both B and C

50. According to the passage, what is auditory occlusion?

  a. Total loss of hearing
  b. Tunnel vision
  c. A temporary loss or lessening of hearing
  d. A sensory disturbance

51. What word below is the best meaning of the word *blatant* as used in paragraph 4?

  a. Obvious
  b. Flagrant
  c. Subtle
  d. Implied

52. In paragraph 2, what is the best synonym for the word *anomaly*?

  a. Common
  b. Strange
  c. Abnormality
  d. Normal

Questions 53-59

Think cattle rustling is a thing of the past? Think again. As of March 2014, cattle rustling in the western United States is still "a thing." Ranchers and law enforcement are diligently working together to protect herds and keep them safe from a brand new threat—meth addicts. People addicted to methamphetamine have turned in their climbing boots and copper wire grabbing gloves to steal cows in order to finance their drug habits. Where's the *Outlaw Josey Wales* when you need him?

Levity aside, neither of the aforementioned issues is a laughing matter. Methamphetamine addiction is very serious, dangerous, and expensive to maintain. Issues surrounding the crime of cow theft is equally serious, dangerous, and expensive. Cows are valuable and can be sold at auction for around $1,000 a head. A local news station obtained video depicting thieves as they stole an entire pen of cows by coaxing them into the back of a big rig in the middle of the night. Another rancher had 100 cows stolen. At $1,000 a head, that's big money, and big jail time. Currently, cattle rustling carries penalties of up to 10 years in prison. The problem for ranchers, while fortuitous for the thieves, is that it's fairly easy to avoid detection while selling stolen livestock at auction. Why? The cows often are not branded.

Why not simply brand the cows? Well, that depends on the rancher. Some ranchers seek support and endorsements from the Certified Humane Project (CHP), and organizations like it, for meat products. CHP grades livestock on a step level from 1 to 5, with 1 being the lowest and 5 being the highest. The higher the meat's rating, the more natural, healthy, and flavorful it is, allowing the farmer to command a premium price. As farmers desire to return to natural and humane ways of farming and cattle raising, while also increasing their earnings potential, fewer farmers are branding their cattle. The more farmers treat their animals humanely and the closer farmers get their animals' habitat to what normally occurs in nature, the higher the farmers score when the meat finally makes it to the grocery stores.

One thing CHP has noted is that branding animals is not humane. As such, ranchers have a decision to make—protect the herd with brands, or resist branding to achieve higher CHP step ratings. Either choice will likely cost them big bucks.

53. What is the main point of this passage?

   a. Cows are expensive
   b. Cattle rustling is still a big problem for ranchers
   c. Ranchers should brand their cows
   d. Meat certifications are big money

54. In paragraph 2, a rancher had 100 cows stolen. According to the article, what is the total monetary loss of the cows before processing?

    a. $1,000,000
    b. $10,000
    c. $100,000
    d. $1,000

55. According to the passage, what is a service that Certified Humane Project provides?

    a. 3rd party evaluation of farms and animal habitat
    b. Rate farms and resultant meat products
    c. Create benchmarks for organic humane food sources
    d. All of the above

56. The passage implies which is true about branding?

    a. Branding hurts the animals
    b. Branding is not an issue
    c. Ranchers make more money if they don't brand
    d. Both A and C

57. The passage mentions each of the following except ______.

    a. Josey Wales
    b. Cattle rustling is big money for addicts
    c. Methamphetamine users used to steal copper to fund their habits
    d. Methamphetamine users need services to help them overcome the addiction.

58. Which of the words below most closely matches the meaning of the word *diligently* as used in the 1st paragraph?

    a. neglectful
    b. persistently
    c. unconcerned
    d. carefully

59. The author's conclusion regarding branding would be most weakened by which of the following?

  a. The ranchers worked with another 3rd party evaluator.
  b. Certified Humane Project worked with ranchers to come to a mutual agreement under the circumstances.
  c. The ranchers in question did not work with the Certified Humane Project.
  d. The ranchers in question decided to start using the brands.

Questions 60-65

After a person convicted of a crime has served a sentence in a jail or prison, he or she is released back into the community. Prisoner release is a source of relief or frustration depending on individual perceptions, experience, and expectations. Some people believe a person who has committed a crime is lost and can never be redeemed. Others believe there are justifiable reasons why any given crime was committed and thus, very few people should go to jail or prison for extended times. Regardless the position, when a person has served a sentence, the person will be released and will return to the community. Moreover, regardless the opinions of others, the released person often has fear, confusion, and apprehension to manage.

So there are many questions that arise. Is it the responsibility of the community to support people who have violated the public trust as they re-enter society? And if so, how do communities support people newly released from jail so they do not become a statistic of recidivism? The answer to these questions forms the basis of re-entry programs throughout the nation.

Generally speaking, most re-entry programs are comprised of various community members and stakeholders. Collaboration between probation, parole, law enforcement, medical and mental health care workers, employment services, housing advocates, clergy, and a host of other services including substance abuse, and domestic violence counseling, are essential for making the transition smooth and successful. Collaborative partners ensure that resources are set up, or in motion, by the time of release so that participants do not find themselves homeless or re-entering a detrimental living situation immediately upon leaving prison.

Re-entry programs have shown success in many communities. However, the perceived level of success may be well above or well below expectations, depending on individual disposition, the attitude of the participant, and the community in which they now live.

60. Based on the tone of this passage, which is it meant to do?

    a. Persuade
    b. Share information
    c. Admonish
    d. Stimulate thought

61. What is an appropriate title for this passage?

    a. Community Frustrated Over Prisoner Release
    b. Prisoner Re-entry Programs: What Happens Next
    c. How to Decrease Recidivism Rates
    d. Prisoner Re-entry

62. Based on the passage, it can be inferred that the author believes which of the following?

    a. Criminals should never be let out of prison.
    b. Many crimes are rational and less people should receive long prison terms.
    c. Community involvement is important for re-entry programs to work well.
    d. Re-entry programs work.

63. As used in the last sentence, what is the best definition of the word *disposition*?

    a. Bad attitude
    b. Frustrations
    c. Positivity
    d. Natural inclination

64. What is the purpose of the second paragraph?

    a. To illustrate the depth of the issue
    b. To pose questions for deeper thinking about the issue
    c. To avoid taking a position
    d. Both A and B

65. Which is the best synonym for the word *redeemed* as used in paragraph 1?

    a. exchanged
    b. converted
    c. reformed
    d. reclaimed

Logical Reasoning

The logical reasoning section measures how well you relate various pieces of information to each other. Information is provided as a group, an ordered series of facts, or sequence of numbers or words. Choose the best answer based on the information provided.

Bonus Questions

66. Suspect A, B, C, and D enter a warehouse intending to steal inventory items. The police arrive and call them out of the warehouse. Suspect A remains inside longer than suspect D. Suspect B comes out first. Suspect C comes out before A but after B. Which suspect is inside the longest?

    a. Suspect B
    b. Suspect D
    c. Suspect A
    d. Suspect C

67. Which suspect came out 3rd?

    a. Suspect A
    b. Suspect D
    c. Suspect C
    d. Not enough information

68. Three of the words below are similar and one is different. Choose the word that is different.

    a. Apple
    b. Pear
    c. Lettuce
    d. Plum

69. If all Widgets are Wing Dings, and some Wing Dings are Blue Bots, then which of the following is true?

    a. All Blue Bots are Widgets
    b. No Wing Dings are Widgets
    c. Some Blue Bots might be Widgets
    d. Some Blue Bots are Wing Dings
    e. Both C and D
    f. None of the Above

Study the sequence of numbers or letters below and complete the sequence.

70. 1, 5, 2, 4, 3, 3, 4, 2, 5, ___

    a. 6
    b. 3
    c. 1
    d. 2

71. 15, 12, 9, __, 3.

    a. 6
    b. 8
    c. 4
    d. 7

72. Carrot, ________, Beet, Turnip, Artichoke

    a. Chard
    b. Radish
    c. Rhubarb
    d. Broccoli

73. 4, 16, 64, ___, 1024
    a. 384
    b. 80
    c. 256
    d. 564

74. If River City can be coded 54 using a specific formula, what would Alamo County be coded using the same formula?

    a. 66
    b. 56
    c. 54
    d. 52

Answer questions 74-75 based on the following information:

The range master must schedule seven range testing dates for the River City annual range program. Each date during the week is coded A, B, C, D, E, F, or G. Seven different consecutive days are available for the range dates and are numbered one through seven in the order that they occur. Only one range date can be scheduled for each day. Additionally, the assignment of the range dates to days during the week is subject to the following restrictions:

I. A and C must occupy consecutive days.
II. A must be scheduled for an earlier day than G.
III. C must be scheduled for a later day than E.
IV. If E does not occupy the fourth day, then D must occupy the fourth day.
V. G and F cannot occupy consecutively numbered days.

75. Which of the following could be a schedule of range dates in the order they occur over the month?

    a. ACDEFBG
    b. BFAECGD
    c. EACDFBG
    d. ECADGFB

76. Which of the following could be true?

    a. A is scheduled on the 1st day
    b. C is scheduled on the 5th day
    c. E is scheduled on the 7th day
    d. F is scheduled on the 6th Day

CLOZE

Questions 77-116

CLOZE

On this part of the test, fill in each blank with the appropriate word. The words are indicated by blank spaces and dashes within the passage. Each dash represents a letter. The word must be correct given the context of the passage, and it must have the same number of letters as dashes. All words that meet both criteria are considered correct. More than one word may be appropriate for a given space.

All law enforcement officers are sworn in to the office using a standard oath. Each new officer proudly swears that _ _ or she will never betray his _ _ her badge, integrity, character or the _ _ _ _ _ _ trust, and to uphold all laws _ _ _ the United States Constitution. Every officer _ _ _ _ _ this oath seriously. Most will never _ _ _ _ _ _ the day that badge was handed _ _ them and they raised their right _ _ _ _ _.

The oath is not the only _ _ _ _ _ _ _ an officer makes every day he _ _ _ _ his badge. At each agency there _ _ _ daily reminders of core values, traditions, _ _ _ _ _ _ _ _ _ rules, the police officers' prayer, and _ _ on. The tenets of each are _ _ _ _ _ _ the same and give an officer _ sense of pride about the job. _ _ _ _ _ _ _ such promise is the police officer _ _ _ _ of ethics. The officer code of _ _ _ _ _ _ takes the promise a little further, _ _ _ _ from the law and toward a _ _ _ _ humanitarian purpose. In the code of _ _ _ _ _ _, an officer affirms his "fundamental duty" _ _ to serve mankind; to defend the _ _ _ _ and defenseless against oppression or intimidation, _ _ _ the peaceful against violence and disorder.

It is this last sentence that _ _ most striking. In the midst of _ _ _ _ _ _ around the nation, many might assume _ _ _ officers' role is to intimidate and _ _ _ _ _ _ _, rather than to prevent. Is _ _ possible then for chaos, violence, and _ _ _ _ _ _ _ _ _ to coexist with peacefulness in the _ _ _ _ space, such that any attempt to _ _ _ _ _ _ _ violence will not necessarily and negatively _ _ _ _ _ _ the peaceful?

And, if so, how _ _ it possible for an officer to _ _ _ _ _ _ to the oath and the code? _ _ _ _ _ _ _, maybe there are two sides to _ _ _ proverbial coin, and both sides of _ _ _ truth are true, even if they _ _ _ seem to conflict. In the meanwhile, _ _ _ can only hope for guidance. We hope also that as we attempt to navigate issues of violence, peace, civil disobedience, and social disorder amid the anger, frustration, and mistrust for one another, each officer will continue to remember the overwhelming pride and honor felt the day that badge was handed to them, they raised their right hand, and swore always to do the right thing.

Practice Exam Answers

Practice Exam One

1. **b.** Answer a is a run on sentence.
2. **a.** Answer b contains a vague reference. The sentence is unclear as to whose supervisor wishes to speak with which employee.
3. **a**. answer b contains a sentence fragment.
4. **b.** Answer a contains a misplaced modifier and is unclear. The sentence can read: Officers who train rarely – are caught off guard. Or: Officers who train – rarely are caught off guard. Answer b is a clearer sentence.
5. **a.** Answer b is a run on sentence.
6. **a**. Answer b contains a sentence fragment.
7. **b.** Answer a contains a sentence fragment.
8. **a**. Answer b is a run on sentence.
9. **b.** Answer a contains a misplaced modifier and is unclear. Choice a as written states "Detective Sherman *almost* got convictions," which implies he got acquittals instead. Choice b is clearer as the word "almost" modifies "every arrest," rather than convictions.
10. **a.** Answer b contains a sentence fragment.
11. **b.** Answer a contains a vague reference and is unclear as to whether it was singing, dancing, acting, or all three that made Kyle happy.
12. **a**. Answer b is a run on sentence.
13. **b**. Answer a contains a misplaced modifier and appears as if "Mary's house" is "happily at work."
14. **a.** Answer b contains a misplaced modifier and is unclear as to whether the officers or the fingerprints are on the print cards.
15. **a.** Answer b contains a vague reference and is unclear as to what Fran kept hidden. "It" relates back to "afraid," indicating it was her *fear* she was hiding. Answer a is more clearly written.
16. **c.** Apathetic means indifferent.
17. **a**. Belligerent means hostile. Answers c and d are not the best answers because a person may be angry or loud without being belligerent.
18. **b**. Callous means insensitive. Answers a and c are not the best answers choices because a person may be mean or annoyed without being callous. Answer d means the opposite.
19. **d.** Hinder means to impede.
20. **b**. Lucid means rational. Answers a and d are the opposite.
21. **a**. Pilfering means stealing.

22. **c**. Inconspicuous means unnoticeable. Answer b means the opposite. Answers a and d are not the best answer choices because both small and large items *could* be inconspicuous.
23. **b**. Intermittent is the opposite of persistent. Answers a and c are synonyms.
24. **c**. Lowers is the opposite of supersede. Answer b is a synonym.
25. **b**. Bolster is the opposite of mitigate. Answer a is a synonym.
26. **b**. In this context, course means manner of procedure. Coarse is a homonym and means harsh or grating.
27. **b**. In this context, serial means producing a series of similar actions, such as killing. Cereal is an edible grain.
28. **a**. Effect as used in this context is a noun. Generally, the word "affect" is a verb, and "effect" is a noun. "Affect" *acts upon* something to cause change such as, "the snow *affected* his ability to drive." "Effect" is *acted upon* and is the result of said act, as in, "the snow had a negative *effect* on the undercarriage of his car." In the exam question, the "increased penalties" had no *effect* on crime.
29. **b**. Hone means to sharpen. Answers a and d are not the *best* choices because, while they are synonyms close in meaning, they are not as close as sharpen.
30. **a**. Repealed means revoked. Answers b and d mean the opposite.
31. **c.** Toward
32. **d.** Liaison
33. **c.** Rescinded
34. **a.** Surprised
35. **b.** Tendency
36. **a.** Necessary
37. **d.** Government
38. **b.** Accommodations
39. **a.** Harassing
40. **c.** Noticeably
41. **d.** Possession
42. **a.** Siege
43. **a**. Publicly
44. **c**. Aggressive
45. **d**. Fluorescent
46. **a**. Objective. The passage is written with an impersonal objective tone, much like an article or news report, rather than to persuade or debate. Thus answers b, c, and d are incorrect.
47. **a**. Absolutely necessary. Imperative in this context means "of vital importance."
48. **d**. I and III only. Option II, which states critical thinking is *only* important in academia, contradicts the entire second paragraph. Be wary of absolutes in multiple-choice exams.
49. **d**. If fewer crimes have been successfully investigated and prosecuted since police began using critical thinking in investigations, then it would appear critical thinking is

not helpful in police work. The purpose of paragraph 3 is to illustrate the many ways critical thinking has been used and can help in law enforcement. Answers a, b, and c are incorrect because they misstate facts or ideas from the passage.

50. **b**. The definition of savvy is shrewd.
51. **b**. Critical Thinking and Law Enforcement. Although the passage defines critical thinking and illustrates its various applications, the bulk of the passage talks about the application of critical thinking to law enforcement. Thus answer b is the best choice.
52. **d**. All of the above. Each point was presented as an important reason critical thinking is used in law enforcement.
53. **d**. The Chief's letter identifies personal reasons why many people cannot schedule exercise into their daily routines. It also mentions the "warriors" that do work out each morning before work, and the liability issues around allowing staff to exercise during shifts. Thus, d is the best answer; the Chief will help, but puts the responsibility on the employee to manage his or her time.
54. **d**. Sarcastic. Though the letter uses mostly cordial words, specific word choices like "warriors," "outlying areas" and "created barriers...to reach...the required baseline goals of this department," lend a disapproving and judgmental tone toward employees who are not exercising regularly due to their own "choices." The Chief begins his letter by applauding employees for wanting to meet standards, but subsequently reprimands them, takes away food choices, and prohibits exercise on meal breaks.
55. **d**. The Chief notes both logistics and liability as reasons why he denied the request.
56. **c**. 9. Paragraph 1 states most officers spend 15 hours a day related to work and commute. There are 24 hours in a day, thus 24 - 15 = 9 hours remaining.
57. **d**. As used in paragraph 3, the Chief implies the "warriors" that work out each morning with him show motivation, energy and a willingness to do what it takes to fit exercise into their schedules.
58. **a**. Technical advancement. Answers c and d are not mentioned or implied in the passage. Answer b relates to how schools are dealing with student safety.
59. **d**. Both A and B. The main point is that bullying has increased in number and scope.
60. **d**. All of the above.
61. **c**. Massive. Monolithic can mean massive or stonelike, but the context of the passage tends to suggest the agency is massive rather than stonelike. Answer d is the opposite.
62. **d**. All of the above
63. **a**. Communication between agencies. The passage mentions the size of various security agencies, among other things, as a reason communication is a problem. Thus answer choice a is the *best* answer.

64. **c**. The passage mentions that varying size and scope of different agencies makes it difficult for them to communicate with one another. If each agency uses its own dedicated communication system, then the systems they use would create the interagency communication problem rather than size and scope of the agencies.
65. **b**. The passage does not make a judgment about any specific type of security agency, thus it can be implied that size and scope do not matter if the operation functions properly.

For Answers 66-70, you should have penciled the following graphic:

VII, VIII and IX, X, and XI = Edward is smallest lot and red, Adam house is white and directly across from Edward; Edward is between Charles and Boy and Charles is directly across from Frank, Frank is green

Charles Blue	Edward Red	Boy
Frank Green	Adam White	

VI = David is largest lot Opposite Yellow

David
Yellow

Adding the two graphics, and deduction that the only remaining color is orange results in:

Charles Blue	Edward Red	Boy Yellow
Frank Green	Adam White	David Orange

VI, VII, XI, Returns from largest to smallest:

David = Largest and Edward = Smallest
Charles is larger than Frank but smaller than Boy and Adam. Boy and Adam are never resolved.

Largest to Smallest Lot Size

1. David
2.
3.
4. Charles
5. Frank
6. Edward

Largest to Smallest Lot Size

1. David
2. Adam/Boy
3. Boy/Adam
4. Charles
5. Frank
6. Edward

66. **b.**
67. **d.**

68. **a.**
69. **d.**
70. **c.**
71. **d**. Train. The other options are all modes of air transportation.

For Answer 72 you should have drawn the following graphic:

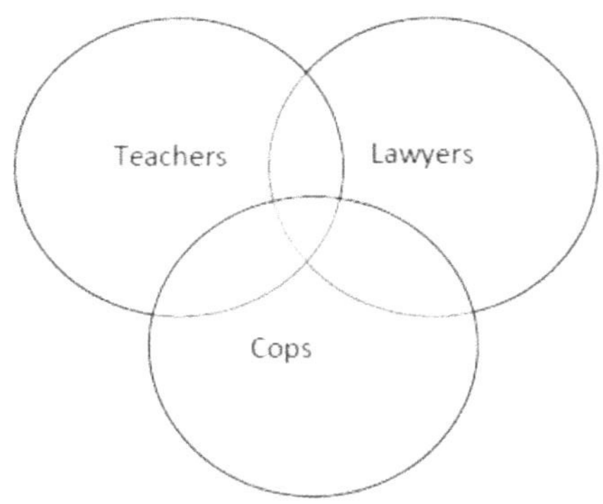

72. **e**. Both c and d. At one point Teachers and Lawyers intersect, and at another Cops, Teachers, and Lawyers all intersect, thus both answer choices c and d are correct. Answer a is incorrect because there is an area of Cops that does not intersect with Lawyers, thus **all** Cops are not Lawyers. Answer b is incorrect because there is clearly an intersection of Cops and Lawyers, thus there are some Cops that are Lawyers. Answer choice b is also disproven by the information presented explicitly in the question.
73. **d.** Banana. Bananas grow on trees, the other choices all grow in the ground.
74. **b.** Deer. The listed items are all mammals and the first letter of each mammal follows the alphabet. Thus, the next item is a mammal beginning with the letter D.
75. **b.** 10. Each number is increased by 2 to return the following number.
76. **b.** Motion. Each word is related to the law or law enforcement and its first letter increases by three letters in alphabetical order. Thus the next word is a law-related word that begins with the letter M.
77. societal
78. more
79. community
80. job
81. job
82. began
83. policing
84. the
85. it
86. job

87. primarily
88. support
89. their
90. to
91. tended
92. communities
93. In
94. resisted
95. work
96. evolved
97. prior
98. Rather
99. then
100. action
101. holding
102. action
103. a
104. stakeholders
105. businesses
106. identify
107. national
108. that
109. and
110. safety
111. disorder
112. based
113. organizational
114. problem
115. systemic
116. response

Practice Exam Two

1. **b.** Sentence a contains a sentence fragment.
2. **b**. Sentence a contains a misplaced modifier and it appears as though Steven's car is "on the way to work."
3. **a.** Sentence b is a run on sentence.
4. **b.** Sentence a contains a vague reference. Officer Daryn says he doesn't like to drive fast, but references an unspecified "you" in the sentence. Sentence b clearly states, it is Officer Daryn who gets sick at high speeds.
5. **b.** Sentence a contains a sentence fragment.
6. **a.** Sentence b contains a vague reference and it is unclear whether the judge or the defendant was remanded into custody.
7. **b.** Sentence a is a run on sentence.
8. **b.** Sentence a contains a vague reference. Jack calls the Sheriff's Office, which is a business comprised of many people, but mentions "they" did not call him back. The use of the pronoun "they" is improper. Sentence b is clearer. An even better way to write this sentence is "Jack called the Sheriff's secretary, but he (or she) did not return Jack's call.
9. **b.** Sentence a contains a sentence fragment.
10. **a.** Sentence b contains a misplaced modifier. It appears Officer Brandt stole the car.
11. **b.** Sentence a is a run on sentence.
12. **b.** Sentence a contains a misplaced modifier. It appears Olivia's vacation was "eagerly awaiting."
13. **b.** Sentence a is a run on sentence.
14. **a.** Sentence b contains a misplaced modifier. It is unclear whether the lunches or the deputies were in bags.
15. **b.** Sentence a contains a vague reference. There is no reference to anything except Alex, who turns on the television in this sentence, thus it is unclear to whom "they" refers. Again, this sentence illustrates an improper use of the pronoun "they."
16. **a**. Frantic means frenzied. Answers c and d are incorrect because it is possible to be frustrated or upset without being frantic.
17. **c**. Exacerbated means aggravated, to make worse. Answer b is the opposite.
18. **d**. Verbose means wordy.
19. **d**. Foster means to promote. Answer c is the opposite.
20. **b**. Supersedes means to override. Answer c is related in meaning but not the best answer. Answer a is opposite.
21. **b**. Dubious means questionable. Answer d is a near opposite. Answers a and c are unrelated in meaning.
22. **a**. Stealthily. Answers c and d are opposites.
23. **b**. Abdicated is the opposite of maintained. Answer d is a synonym. Answers a and c are near but unrelated.

24. **d**. Deviate is the opposite of remain. Answers a, b, and c are synonyms.
25. **c**. Guile is the opposite of honesty. Answer a is a synonym. Answer d is close, but unrelated in meaning given the context.
26. **a**. Incite means to "urge on." Insight is the ability to see an underlying truth.
27. **a**. Know means to have knowledge. No is used to show dissent or denial.
28. **b**. Steal means to take another's property without permission. Steel is a type of metal.
29. **b**. Affable means friendly.
30. **b**. Alienated means estranged. Answer d is the opposite.
31. **a**. Adversarial
32. **d**. Germane
33. **b**. Palpable
34. **c**. Subpoena
35. **d**. Suspicious
36. **c**. Facilitate
37. **a**. Heinous
38. **d**. Incorrigible
39. **b**. Perfunctory
40. **a**. Seditious
41. **b**. Surveillance
42. **a**. Tenacious
43. **d**. Vagrancy
44. **a**. Interrogated
45. **b**. Independent
46. **b.** Witnesses can be unreliable. Answers a, c, and d are *reasons* witnesses can be unreliable.
47. **a.** Officers must diligently investigate due to witness unreliability.
48. **d.** All of the above
49. **d.** Both b and c
50. **c.** A temporary loss or lessening of hearing
51. **b.** Blatant means flagrant. Answer a is close in meaning but is not the *best* answer. Answer c is the opposite.
52. **c.** Anomaly means abnormality. Answer b is close in meaning but not the *best* answer. Answers a and d are antonyms.
53. **b.** Cattle rustling is still a big problem for ranchers.
54. **c.** $100, 000. 100 cows multiplied by $1,000 per cow.
55. **d.** All of the above
56. **d.** Both a and c
57. **d.** Methamphetamine users need services to help overcome addiction.
58. **b**. Diligently means persistently.

59. **c.** If the ranchers in question did not work with the CHP, then the CHP's standards regarding branding would have no bearing on the ranchers' income or subsequent decision whether to brand.
60. **d.** The main point of the passage is to stimulate thought. Answer b is incorrect because the passage does more than simply provide information. Answers a and c are incorrect because the passage is objective in its presentation of information and opinion.
61. **b.** Answer c is incorrect because the passage does not mention how to decrease recidivism. Answer a is incorrect because it is a supporting point. Answer d is incorrect because it is vague.
62. **c.** Answers a and b are differing opinions explicitly stated in the passage. Answer d is misstated. Answer c is the best choice since the passage discusses the value of collaboration among community stakeholders.
63. **d**. Natural inclination. Answers a, b, and c are incorrect because each can be a natural inclination.
64. **d**. Both a and b
65. **c**. Redeem means to buy back, recover, exchange or reform. In this context, *redeemed* means reformed.
66. **c.** Suspect A comes out last.
67. **d.** Either Suspect C or Suspect D could have come out 3rd. There is not enough information to determine this answer.
68. **c.** Lettuce is a vegetable and the remaining choices are fruits.

For Answer 68 you should have drawn the following graphic:

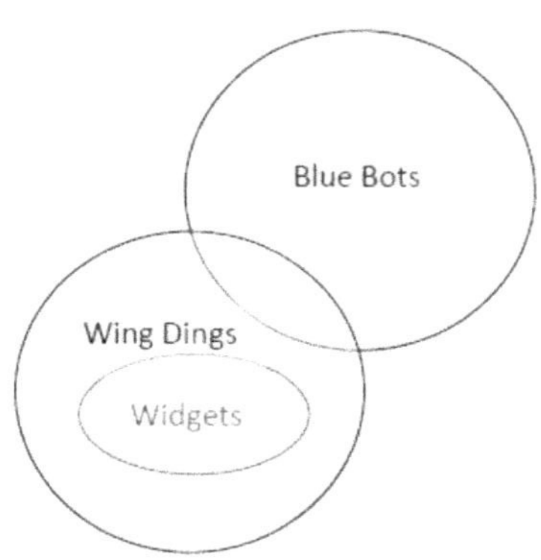

69. **e**. Both c and d. Answer a is incorrect because it is possible for some Blue Bots to be Blue Bots only, and therefore not Widgets. Answer b is incorrect because if *all* Widgets are Wing Dings, then *some* Wing Dings are Widgets.
70. **c**. Every other number increases or decreases by one. Starting with the first number, every other number *increases* by one: 1, 2, 3, 4, 5. Starting with the second number, every other number *decreases* by one: 5, 4, 3, 2, thus the next number in the sequence is 1.

71. **a.** 6. Beginning with the first number, each successive number decreases by 3.
72. **c.** Rhubarb. Each word is a vegetable. Beginning with the first word, each successive word begins with the 4th letter of the preceding word. Thus, the missing word must begin with the letter "R" and contain the letter "b" as its 4th letter.
73. **c.** 256. Beginning with the first number, each successive number is multiplied by 4: 4 x 64 is 256.
74. **b.** 56. The code is determined by the total number of letters in each word. The word "River" contains 5 letters and "City" contains 4 letters, thus the code for River City is 54. The word "Alamo" contains 5 letters and "County" contains 6 letters, thus the code for Alamo County is 56.
75. **c**. EACDFBG. Answer a is incorrect because range date C comes before E, in violation of condition III. Answer b is incorrect because range dates A and C are not consecutive, in violation of condition I. Answer d is incorrect because range dates G and F are consecutive, in violation of condition V.
76. **b**. C is scheduled on the 5th day. Answer a is incorrect because under these conditions, range date C must follow. Since range date C must come after range date E per condition III, if range date A is first, condition III can't be met. Answer c is incorrect because if range date E is last, it cannot come before range date C, which violates condition III. Answer d is incorrect because if range date F is on the 6th day then range date G must be on the 4th day, in violation of condition IV.
77. he
78. or
79. public
80. and
81. takes
82. forget
83. to
84. hands
85. promise
86. dons
87. are
88. cardinal
89. so
90. fairly
91. a
92. Another
93. code
94. ethics
95. away
96. more
97. ethics
98. is

99. weak
100. and
101. is
102. unrest
103. the
104. oppress
105. it
106. disorder
107. same
108. address
109. affect
110. is
111. adhere
112. However
113. the
114. the
115. may
116. one

Appendix A: Commonly Misspelled Words

This reference guide is adapted to reflect commonly misspelled words that are related to law enforcement. It outlines the word as correctly spelled, followed by the common misspellings and tips to ensure proper spelling.

See the section on spelling tips and tricks for a more in-depth explanation of various spelling tips.

Correct spelling	Common misspelling	Tip
accommodate, accommodation	accomodate, accomodation	double up the **c**s, and **m**s
acceptable	aceptible, acceptible	has two **c**s and remember, you are **able** to accept
acquire and acquit	aquit, aquire	add a **c** before **qu**
aggressive, aggression	agressive, agression	spelled with two **g**s
apparently	apparently	**-ent** not –ant
appearance	appearence	ends with **–ance** not ence
assassination	assasination	two sets of double **s**, like Mississippi
basically	basicly	ends with **–ally**
beginning	begining	add an **n** before adding the **-ing**
bizarre	bizzare	spelled with one **z**, and two **r**s
calendar	calender	ends with -**ar** not -**er**
colleague	collegue	the second half is **league**, like baseball
completely	completly	don't drop the **e** and add **ly;** ends with -**ely**
conscious	concious	spelled with an **s** and **c** in the middle
definitely	definately	spelled with **ite,** not ate
dilemma	dilemna	double **m**
disappear	dissapear	spelled with one **s**, and two **p**s
disappoint	dissapoint	spelled with one **s**, and two **p**s
discipline	disapline	spelled with an **s** and **c** in the middle; **i** instead of **a**
embarrass	embarass	double up **r** and **s**
environment	enviroment	an **n** comes before the **m**
existence	existance	ends with **-ence**
finally	finaly	spelled with two **l**s
fluorescent	florescent	begins with **fluor** and ends with **scent**
foreign	foriegn	**e** before **i**, an exception to the "**ie**" rule

foreseeable	forseeable	begins with **fore**, not for
forty	fourty	begins with **for**, not four
forward	foward	begins with **for**, not fo
further	futher	begins with **fur**, not fu
gist	jist	begins with **g**
government	goverment	there is an **n** before the **m**
harass, harassment	harrass, harrassment	spelled with one **r**, and two **s**'s
idiosyncrasy	idiosyncracy	ends with **-asy** not -acy
incidentally	incidently	ends with **-ally**
independent	independant	ends with **-ent** not -ant
interrupt	interupt	spelled with two **r**s
irresistible	irresistable	ends with **-ible**
knowledge	knowlege	remember the silent **d**
liaise, liaison	liase, liason	there is an **i** before and after the **a**: **iai**
necessary	neccessary	spelled with one **c** and two **s**'s
noticeable	noticable	do not drop the **e** when adding **-able**
occasion	ocassion, occassion	spelled with two **c**s and one **s**
occurred, occurring	occured, occuring	spelled with two **c**s and two **r**s
occurrence	occurance, occurence	spelled with two **c**s and two **r**s, and ends with **-ence** not -ance
persistent	persistant	ends with **-ent** not -ant
possession	posession	two sets of double **s** like Mississippi
preferred, preferring	prefered, prefering	the second **r** is doubled
publicly	publically	simply add **ly** to the end of public
recommend	recomend	spelled with two **m**s
referred, referring	refered, refering	the second **r** is doubled
reference	referance	Ends with -**ence** not -ance
relevant	relevent	ends with -**ant** not -ent
resistance	resistence	ends with **-ance**
sense	sence	ends with **-se**
separate	seperate	spelled with **-par-** in the middle
siege	seige	**i** before **e** rule
successful	succesful	double up the **c**s and **s**'s
supersede	supercede	ends with **sede**
surprise	suprise	begins with **sur**, not su
tendency	tendancy	ends with **-ency** not -ancy
tomorrow	tommorow, tommorrow	spelled with one **m** and two **r**s
tongue	tounge	begins with **ton-** and ends with **-gue**
unforeseen	unforseen	spelled with an **e** after the **r**

unfortunately	unfortunatly	don't drop the **e** when adding **ly**
until	untill	spelled with one **l** at the end
weird	wierd	**e** before **i**, an exception to the **ie** rule

Appendix B: Spelling/Vocabulary Words Related to Law Enforcement

A

1. **Abdicate** -(verb) to cast off, renounce, or relinquish
2. **Aberrant** -(noun) a state or condition markedly different from the norm
3. **Abject** -(adj.)sunk to a low condition or in miserable circumstances
4. **Abolish** -(verb) do away with
5. **Abide** -(verb) accept or act in accordance with (a rule, decision, or recommendation)
6. **Abridge** -(verb) lessen, diminish, or curtail; reduce in scope while retaining essential elements
7. **Accolade** -(noun) a tangible symbol signifying approval or distinction
8. **Accomplice** -(noun) a person who joins with another in carrying out some plan (especially an unethical or illegal plan)
9. **Accord** -(verb) agreement, harmony
10. **Acquiesce** -(verb) to agree or express agreement; rest satisfied
11. **Acumen** -(noun) shrewdness shown by keen insight
12. **Adversary** - (noun) someone who offers opposition
13. **Affable** -(adj.) friendly; outgoing disposition
14. **Affect** -(verb) act on; produce an effect or change in
15. **Affirmation** -(noun) a statement asserting the existence or the truth of something
16. **Alienate** -(verb) make hostile or indifferent
17. **Allegation** –(noun) (law) a formal accusation against somebody
18. **Alleviate** -(verb) provide physical relief, as from pain; make easier
19. **Aloof** -(adj.) remote in manner; distant
20. **Amass** -(verb) collect or gather; get or gather together
21. **Ambiguous** -(adj.) having more than one possible meaning; often misleading
22. **Ambivalence** -(noun) mixed feelings or emotions
23. **Ambulatory** -(adj.) relating to or adapted for walking; able to walk about
24. **Antagonize** -(verb) provoke the hostility of; act in opposition to
25. **Apathy** -(noun) lacking enthusiasm for or interest in things generally; an absence of enthusiasm; indifference
26. **Assailant** -(noun) a person who attacks violently (with blows or words)
27. **Assault** -(verb) a threatened or attempted physical attack by someone who appears to be able to cause bodily harm if not stopped
28. **Assignment** -(noun) a duty that you are assigned to perform (especially in the armed forces)
29. **Augment** -(verb) enlarge or increase; grow or intensify

B

30. **Belie** -(verb) represent falsely; be in contradiction with
31. **Belittle** -(verb) lessen the authority, dignity, or reputation of; cause to seem less serious
32. **Belligerence** -(noun) hostile or warlike attitude or nature; a natural disposition to be hostile

33. **Benign** -(adj.) pleasant and beneficial in nature or influence; kindness of disposition or manner; not dangerous to health
34. **Bizarre** -(adj.) conspicuously or grossly unconventional or unusual
35. **Blatant** -(adj.) noisy in a vulgar or offensive manner
36. **Brevity -**(noun) the attribute of being brief or fleeting; the use of brief expressions

C

37. **Cajole** -(verb) to deceive or persuade with false pretenses
38. **Callous** -(verb) make insensitive or callous; deaden feelings or morals; (adj.) emotionally hardened
39. **Candid** -(adj.) openly straightforward and direct without reserve or secretiveness; informal or natural
40. **Capitulate** -(verb) surrender under agreed conditions
41. **Censure** -(noun) harsh criticism or disapproval; the state of being excommunicated; (verb) rebuke formally
42. **Clemency** -(noun) leniency and compassion shown toward offenders of rule or law
43. **Coalesce** -(verb) fuse or cause to grow together; mix together different elements
44. **Coerce** -(verb) force by using pressure, intimidation, or threats
45. **Collusion** -(verb) secret agreement or cooperation
46. **Commission** -(noun) the act of committing
47. **Complacent** -(adj.) contented to a fault with oneself or one's actions
48. **Compliant** -(adj.) complying, obeying, yielding
49. **Confide** -(verb) reveal in private; tell confidentially; confer a trust upon
50. **Confound** -(verb) mistake one thing for another; be confusing or perplexing to
51. **Conspiracy** -(noun) a secret agreement between two or more people to perform an unlawful act
52. **Contaminant** -(noun) a substance that violates the purity of an item
53. **Contempt** -(noun) a willful disobedience to or disrespect for the authority of a court or legislative body
54. **Controversial** -(adj.) marked by or capable of arousing controversy
55. **Converge** -(verb) come together so as to form a single product; move or draw together at a certain location
56. **Copious** -(adj.) large in number or quantity; affording an abundant supply
57. **Corroborate** -(verb) support with evidence or authority or make more certain or confirm; establish or strengthen as with new evidence or facts
58. **Corrupt** -(verb) alter from the original; (adj.) lacking in integrity
59. **Counterfeit** -(noun) a copy that is represented as the original, not genuine
60. **Cursory** -(adj.) hasty and without attention to detail; not thorough
61. **Credence** -(noun) the attitude that something is believable and should be accepted as true
62. **Cryptic** -(adj.) having a puzzling terseness; of an obscure nature; having a secret or hidden meaning

D

63. **Debilitate** - (verb) make weak
64. **Delinquency** - (noun) an antisocial misdeed in violation of the law by a minor

65. **Delusion** -(noun) deception by creating illusory ideas; a mistaken or unfounded opinion or idea
66. **Deplete** -(verb) use or exhaust resources
67. **Derelict** -(adj.) abandoned duty or neglected by owner or occupant
68. **Deviate** -(verb) to stray from the norm or standard
69. **Detain** -(verb) deprive of freedom
70. **Discrepancy** -(noun) a difference between conflicting facts or claims or opinions; an event that departs from expectations
71. **Disdain** -(noun) lack of respect accompanied by a feeling of intense dislike; (verb) reject with contempt
72. **Disingenuous** -(adj.) not straightforward or candid; giving a false appearance of frankness
73. **Docile** -(adj.) easily handled or managed; ready and willing to be taught
74. **Dubious** -(adj.) not convinced; fraught with uncertainty or doubt; open to doubt or suspicion

E

75. **Edict** -(noun) a proclamation having the force of law
76. **Effect** -(noun) (of a law) having legal validity
77. **Encumber** -(verb) to weigh down or burden (with difficulties, cares, debt, etc.); to fill up, block up, hinder
78. **Entail** -(verb) to put a burden on, impose, require, involve; to restrict ownership of property by limiting inheritance; (noun) such a restriction
79. **Equilibrium** -(noun) a stable, balanced system
80. **Equivocate** -(verb) be deliberately ambiguous or unclear in order to mislead or withhold information
81. **Evanescent** -(adj.) tending to vanish like vapor
82. **Exacerbate** -(verb) exasperate or irritate; make worse
83. **Exclusionary** -(noun) act of excluding
84. **Exculpate** -(verb) to clear from fault or guilt
85. **Exonerate** -(verb) pronounce not guilty of criminal charges
86. **Expedite** -(verb) process fast and efficiently; speed up the progress of; facilitate
87. **Expendable** -(adj.) able to be spent or done away with

F

88. **Facilitate** -(verb) make easier; increase the likelihood of (a response); be of use
89. **Fathom** -(noun) understanding or comprehension; also a unit of length equal to 6 cubic feet; (verb) to penetrate to the meaning or nature of; comprehend; to determine the depth of (in lengths of six feet) - sound as in "fathoming the ocean."
90. **Flourish** -(verb) grow stronger; move or swing back and forth; gain in wealth
91. **Forfeiture** -(noun) the act of forfeiting
92. **Foster** -(verb) help develop, help grow
93. **Frantic** -(adj.) emotionally out of control
94. **Fraud** -(noun) intentional deception resulting in injury to another person
95. **Fraudulent** -(adj.) intended to deceive

96. **Furtive** -(adj.) marked by quiet and caution and secrecy; taking pains to avoid being observed; secret and sly or sordid
97. **Futile** -(adj.) producing no result or effect; unproductive of success

G

98. **Garner** -(verb) store grain; assemble or get together; acquire or deserve by one's efforts or actions
99. **Germane** -(adj.) relevant or appropriate
100. **Glean** -(verb) gather, as of natural products; to pick over in search of relevant materials
101. **Grievance** -(noun) an allegation that something imposes an illegal obligation or denies some legal right or causes injustice
102. **Guarantee** -(noun) a written assurance that some product or service will be provided or will meet certain specifications
103. **Guile** -(noun) the use of tricks to deceive someone; the quality of being deceitful

H

104. **Harassment** -(verb) the act of tormenting by continued persistent attacks and criticism
105. **Heinous** -(adj.) very wicked, offensive, hateful
106. **Hinder** -(verb) put at a disadvantage
107. **Hone** -(verb) make perfect or complete; sharpen
108. **Hypocritical** -(adj.) professing feelings or virtues one does not have

I

109. **Immunity** -(noun) the state of not being susceptible
110. **Impression** -(noun) a feeling or understanding resulting from an experience
111. **Imprison** -(verb) lock up or confine, in or as in a jail
112. **Incite** -(verb) to provoke
113. **Inconspicuous** -(adj.) not prominent or readily noticeable
114. **Incorrigible** -(adj.) impervious to correction by punishment
115. **Incriminating** -(adj.) charging or suggestive of guilt or blame
116. **Indictment** -(noun) a formal document written for a prosecuting attorney charging a person with some offense
117. **Indignant** -(adj.) angered at something unjust or wrong
118. **Initiative** -(noun) the first of a series of actions
119. **Innocuous** -(adj.) producing no injury; harmless
120. **Insolent** -(adj.) unrestrained by convention or propriety; marked by casual disrespect
121. **Integrity** -(noun) honesty, high moral standards; an unimpaired condition, completeness, soundness
122. **Ironic** -(adj.) characterized by often poignant differences or incongruity between what is expected and what actually is; humorously sarcastic or mocking
123. **Irrefutable** -(adj.) impossible to deny or disprove

J

124. **Jeopardize** -(verb) to expose to danger or risk

125. **Judicial** -(noun) relating to the administration of justice or the function of a judge
126. **Judiciary** -(noun) the system of law courts that administer justice and constitute the judicial branch of government
127. **Judicious** -(adj.) marked by the exercise of good judgment or common sense in practical matters
128. **Jurisdiction** -(noun) (law) the right and power to interpret and apply the law
129. **Juvenile** -(noun) of or relating to or characteristic of or appropriate for children or young people
130. **Juxtapose** -(verb) place side by side

K

L

131. **Legitimate** -(adj.) authorized, sanctioned by, or in accordance with law
132. **Leniency** -(noun) lightening a penalty or excusing from a chore by judges or parents or teachers; a disposition to yield to the wishes of someone; mercifulness as a consequence of being lenient or tolerant
133. **License** -(noun) the act of giving a formal (usually written) authorization
134. **Listless** -(adj.) lacking zest or vivacity; marked by low spirits; showing no enthusiasm
135. **Lucid** -(adj.) having a clear mind; transparently clear; easily understandable; transmitting light; able to be seen through with clarity; capable of thinking and expressing yourself in a clear and consistent manner; rational

M

136. **Maintain** -(verb) keep in safety and protect from harm, decay, loss, or destruction
137. **Mayhem** -(noun) deliberate injury of someone, especially maiming; a state of violent chaos
138. **Miscreant** -(noun) a person without moral scruples
139. **Mitigate** -(verb) make less severe or harsh; to lessen the seriousness or extent of
140. **Morbid** -(adj.) suggesting an unhealthy mental state; caused by or altered by or manifesting disease or pathology; suggesting the horror of death and decay
141. **Mundane** -(adj.) ordinary, often boring
142. **Myriad** -(noun) a large indefinite number, (adj.) too numerous to be counted

N

143. **Narcissistic** -(adj.) characteristic of those having an inflated idea of their own importance; often selfish
144. **Nebulous** -(adj.) lacking definition or definite content; lacking definite form or limits
145. **Nefarious** -(adj.) extremely wicked
146. **Negligible** -(adj.) so small as to be meaningless; insignificant; not worth considering
147. **Nexus** -(noun) a connected series or group; the means of connection between things linked in series
148. **Nonchalant** -(adj.) marked by blithe unconcern
149. **Nullify** -(verb) make ineffective by counterbalancing the effect of; show to be invalid; declare invalid
150. **Negligent** -(adj.) characterized by neglect and undue lack of concern

151. **Nuisance** -(noun) (law) a broad legal concept including anything that disturbs the reasonable use of your property or endangers life and health or is offensive

O

152. **Oblivion** -(noun) the state of being disregarded or forgotten; total forgetfulness
153. **Obscure** -(verb) make difficult to perceive by sight; (adj.) not clearly understood or expressed
154. **Onus** -(noun) an onerous or difficult concern

P

155. **Pacify** -(verb) fight violence and try to establish peace; cause to be more favorably inclined; gain the goodwill of
156. **Palpable** -(adj.) capable of being perceived by the senses or the mind; especially capable of being handled or felt
157. **Pejorative** -(adj.) derogatory or demeaning
158. **Perfunctory** -(adj.) hasty and without attention to detail; not thorough; as a formality only
159. **Peripheral** -(adj.) the outer area; related to the key issue but not of central importance
160. **Petulant** -(adj.) easily irritated or annoyed
161. **Pilfer** -(verb) make off with belongings of others; steal
162. **Placate** -(verb) to soothe or mollify
163. **Precedent** -(noun) (civil law) a law established by following earlier judicial decisions
164. **Pretentious** -(adj.) making claim to or creating an appearance of importance or distinction; intended to attract notice and impress others; of a display that is tawdry or vulgar
165. **Prevalent** -(adj.)widely accepted, favored, or practiced
166. **Proclivity** -(noun) a natural inclination
167. **Profuse** -(adj.) produced or growing in extreme abundance
168. **Provoke** -(verb) provide the needed stimulus for; evoke or provoke to appear or occur; call forth emotions or feelings
169. **Proximity** -(noun) the property of being close together
170. **Provision** -(noun) the activity of supplying or providing something
171. **Prevaricate** -(verb) to speak falsely or misleadingly, deliberately misstate, or create an incorrect impression

Q

172. **Queasy** -(adj.) causing or fraught with or showing anxiety; feeling nausea; feeling about to vomit
173. **Quell** -(verb) To calm; pacify; to put an end to; to allay or quiet
174. **Quirk** -(noun) a strange habit; (verb) twist or curve abruptly

R

175. **Recalcitrant** -(adj.) marked by stubborn resistance to authority; stubbornly resistant to authority or control
176. **Recant** -(verb) formally reject or disavow a formerly held belief, usually under pressure
177. **Reciprocal** -(adj.) shared or felt on both sides
178. **Reclusive** -(adj.) providing privacy or seclusion; withdrawn from society; seeking solitude
179. **Redress** -(noun) a sum of money paid in compensation for loss or injury
180. **Refute** -(verb) to disprove; to successfully argue against
181. **Repeal** -(verb) revoke; annul
182. **Replete** -(verb) fill to satisfaction; (adj.) filled or permeated; filled to satisfaction with food or drink
183. **Reprobate** -(noun) depraved, unprincipled, wicked person
184. **Rescind** -(verb) annul by recalling or rescinding
185. **Resolute** -(adj.) firm in purpose or belief; characterized by firmness and determination
186. **Respite** -(noun) a pause from doing something; a pause for relaxation; the act of reprieving

S

187. **Sabotage** -(verb) an action taken to destroy something or to prevent it from working properly; to take such destructive action
188. **Sanction** -(verb) give authority or permission to
189. **Savvy** -(adj.) shrewd
190. **Scrutinize** -(verb) examine carefully for accuracy with the intent of verification; to look at critically or searchingly, or in minute detail
191. **Seditious** -(adj.) in opposition to a civil authority or government; arousing to action or rebellion
192. **Sovereign** -(noun) a nation's ruler or head of state usually by hereditary right; (adj.) greatest in status or authority or power; not controlled by outside forces
193. **Stringent** -(adj.) demanding strict attention to rules and procedures
194. **Subtle** -(adj.) faint and difficult to analyze; able to make fine distinctions
195. **Subdue** -(verb) correct by punishment or discipline, put down by force or intimidation
196. **Succinct** -(adj.) briefly giving the gist of something
197. **Suppress** -(verb) to put down by force or authority
198. **Surveillance** -(verb) close observation of a person or group (usually by the police)
199. **Speculation** -(noun) a hypothesis that has been formed by speculating or conjecturing (usually with little hard evidence)
200. **Statute** -(noun) an act passed by a legislative body

T

201. **Tantamount** -(adj.) being essentially equal to something in value or significance
202. **Tenacious** -(adj.) sticking together; good at remembering; stubbornly unyielding
203. **Tenuous** -(adj.) very thin in gauge or diameter; having thin consistency; having little substance or significance
204. **Tranquil** -(adj.) free from agitation or worry; calm
205. **Transient** -(noun) in physics, a short-lived oscillation in a system caused by a sudden change of voltage or current or load; lasting a very short time

206. **Thwart** -(verb) to oppose successfully; to prevent, frustrate

U

207. **Usurp** -(verb) to seize or hold in possession by force without right

V

208. **Vagrancy** -(noun) the state or condition of being a vagrant
209. **Verbose** -(adj.) using or containing too many words
210. **Vilification** -(noun) a rude expression intended to offend or hurt; slanderous defamation

W

211. **Warrant** -(noun) a writ from a court commanding police performance of specified acts
212. **Wary** -(adj.) marked by keen caution and watchful prudence; openly distrustful and unwilling to confide
213. **Willful** -(adj.) habitually disposed to disobedience and opposition; done by design

X

Y

Z

214. **Zeal** -(noun) excessive fervor to do something or accomplish some end
215. **Zealot** -(noun) a fervent and even militant proponent of something
216. **Zealous** -(adj.) marked by active interest and enthusiasm

Appendix C: Root Words and Affixes

The following is a reference guide to common Greek and Latin root words, as well as common prefixes and suffixes.

For more information on understanding prefixes, suffixes, and root words, see the vocabulary section of the review guide.

Common Latin and Greek Roots

Latin Root	Definition	Examples
actus, act	drive, lead, act	active, activism, activate, react
acurer	to sharpen	acute, acumen, acuity
ambi	both	ambiguous, ambidextrous
aqua	water	aquarium, aquatic
arbit	judge	arbitrary, arbitration
aud	to hear	audience, audible, auditory
bene	good	benevolent, beneficial
caedere, cide	to cut, kill	incision, pesticide, homicide
capere, cip, cept	take, seize	captive, capture, captivate, intercept
cedere, ced, ceed	to go, yield	recede, precede, exceed, predecessor
circum	around	circumference, circumvent, circumscribe
contra, counter	against	contradict, contrary, counteract
credere, cred	to believe, to trust	credit, credential, credibility, credence
dict	to say	dictation, dictate, predict
duc, duct	to lead	conduct, induce, induct
equis, equ, iqu	equal, even	equidistant, inequity, equivalent, equitable
errare, err, errat	wander, go astray	errant, err, erratic, aberration
fac	to do, to make	factory, manufacture, artifact

finis, fin	end, limit	final, definite, infinite
form	shape	conform, reform
fort	strength	fortitude, fortress, fortify, comfort
fract	to break	fracture, fraction
gravis, grav, griev	heavy, serious	grave, grievance, grievous, aggravate, gravity
ject	throw	eject, project, reject
jud	judge	judicial, prejudice
jus, jur, just	right, law, oath	abjure, perjury, conjure, jury, jurisprudence
mal	bad	malevolent, malfeasance, malcontent
mater	mother	maternal, maternity
mit	to send	transmit, admit, emit
mort	death	mortal, mortician, immortal, mortify
multi	many	multimedia, multiple, multiply, multicolored
onus, oner	burden	onerous, onus, exonerate
pater	father	paternal, paternity
port	to carry	portable, transportation, export
pretiare, prec	to value	precious, deprecation, depreciation, appreciation
rupt	to break	bankrupt, disrupt, erupt
scrib, scribe	to write	inscribe, prescribe, describe
sect, sec	to cut	bisect, section, intersect, dissect
senteire, sent	to feel, perceive, to send	consent, resent, sentient, dissent
spect	to look	inspect, spectator, circumspect, retrospective
struct	to build	construct, destruct, restructure, infrastructure
tacere, tac, tic	to be silent	tacit, taciturn, reticent

tendere, tend	stretch, extend, tend	contend, extend, distend
terrere, terr	frighten	deter, terror, terrorism
venire, veni, ven	come, move toward	convention, contravene, intervene
vid, vis	to see	video, envision, evident, vision
voc	voice, to call	vocalize, advocate, equivocate

Greek Root	**Definition**	**Examples**
agon	contest, struggle	antagonist, agony
anthropo	man, human, humanity	anthropologist, philanthropist
archos, arch	chief, first, rule	monarch, archangel, anarchy
auto	self	autobiography, autocrat, autoimmune, autograph
bio	life	biology, biography
chron	time	chronological, chronic, synchronize
(k) clino, clin	lean, slant	incline, decline, inclination, recline
crit	judge	criticize, critical
crypto, crypt	hide, conceal	cryptic, cryptogram, encryption
dyna	power	dynamic, dynamite, dynamo
dys	bad, hard, unlucky	dysfunctional, dyslexic, dystopia
gno, gnos	know	diagnosis, ignore, incognito, cognitive
gram	thing written	telegram, diagram, grammar
graph	writing	graphic, phonograph
hetero	different	heteronym, heterogeneous
homo	same	homonym, homogenous
hydr	water	hydrate, dehydrate, hydraulic

hypo	below, beneath	hypothermia, hypothetical, hypoglycemic
logy	study of	biology, psychology, sociology
meter, metr	measure	thermometer, perimeter, metric
micro	small	microbe, microscope, microchip
mis, miso	hate, wrong	misanthrope, misogyny, misbehave
mono	one	monologue, monotonous, monotheism
morph	form, shape	morphology, metamorphosis
nom	rule	anomaly, anomalous
nym	name	antonym, synonym, homonym
opsis, optic	sight, eye, view	optical, synopsis
phil	love	philanthropist, philosophy
phobia	fear	claustrophobia, acrophobia, phobic
phon	sound	cacophony, phonetic, symphony
photo, phos	light	photograph, photogenic, phosphorous
pseudo	false	pseudonym, pseudoscience
psycho	soul, spirit	psychology, psychic, psychotic
scope	to watch, see	microscope, telescope
skep, scop	examine	skeptical, scope
techno	art, science, skill	technique, technological
tele	far off	television, telephone, teleport
therm	heat	thermal, thermometer, thermos
thesis	position	synthesis, thesis
zelos	ardor, zeal	zealous, zealot

Common Prefixes

Prefix	Definition	Examples
ambi-, amb-	around, on both sides	ambiguous, ambivalent
anti-	against, opposite	anticlimactic, antibody, antiseptic
bi-	two	bifurcate, bicentennial, biped
circum-, circa-	around, about	circumference, circa, circumvent
con-	against	contrary, contradict
de-	reduce, remove	devalue, decelerate, decompose
di/s-	not, opposite of	discover, digress, disappear
en-, em-	cause to, into	enact, empower, embrace, enclose
fore-	before, front of	foreshadow, forebear, forgo
in-, im-	in, into	income, impulse, innovate
in-, im-, il-, ir-	not, without	indirect, immoral, illegal, irresponsible
inter-	between, among	interrupt, intercept, intercede
mid-	middle	midfield, midterm, midway
mis-	wrong, bad, hate	misspell, misnomer, misanthrope
non-	not, without	nonviolent, nonconformist, nonfiction
over-	excessive	overeat, overstock, overconfident
peri-	around, about	periphery, perimeter
pre-	before	preview, precedent, precept
re-, red-	again, back, against, behind	rewrite, relegate, redeem
semi-	half, partial	semifinal, semiconscious, semicircle
sub-	under	subway, submerge, submarine

super-	above, beyond	superhuman, superfluous, superior
trans-	across, over, through, beyond	transmit, transgression, transit
un-	not, opposite of	unusual, unashamed, unfair

Common Suffixes

Suffix	Definition	Examples
-able, -ible	is, can be	affordable, sensible, unalienable
-al, -ial	having characteristics of, pertaining to	universal, facial, ephemeral
-ed	past tense	called, treated, arrested
-en	made of, to cause to be	golden, darken, frighten
-er, -or	a person who	professor, volunteer
-er	more	taller, shorter, meaner
-est	the most	fastest, shortest, meanest
-ful	full of	helpful, shameful, thankful
-ic	relating, having characteristics of	poetic, dogmatic, organic
-ing	present participles, materials	sleeping, eating, bedding, frosting
-ion, -tion, -ation, -sion	act, process	submission, celebration, navigation
-ity, -ty	state of, condition	activity, society, civility, abnormality
-ive, -ative, -itive	quality of	active, repulsive, sensitive
-less	without	hopeless, homeless, remorseless
-ly	in the manner of	lovely, courageously, horrifically
-ment	state of being, act of	contentment, resentment, placement
-ness	state of, condition of	weakness, kindness
-ous, -eous, -ious	having qualities of, full of	riotous, righteous, hazardous
-y	characterized by	sassy, cheeky, slimy

CPSIA information can be obtained
at www.ICGtesting.com
Printed in the USA
LVHW011336290519
618341LV00038B/367/P

9 781941 759240